Fishing the Wilder Shores

SIDNEY SPENCER
Fishing the Wilder Shores

An anthology of his writing on lake fishing
for trout, sea trout and salmon

EDITED AND INTRODUCED BY
JEREMY LUCAS

H. F. & G. WITHERBY LTD

First published as a collection in 1991 by
H. F. & G. Witherby Ltd
14 Henrietta Street, London WC2E 8QJ

A CIP catalogue record for this book
is available from the British Library

ISBN 0 85493 208 9

Typeset by CentraCet, Cambridge
Printed in Great Britain by
St Edmundsbury Press Ltd, Bury St Edmunds, Suffolk

Contents

Contents

Fishing the Wilder Shores

Introduction
by Jeremy Lucas

━━━━━━━━━━━━━

I feel that I have been poaching into a man's life. Voyeurish, I have leafed through private correspondence and intimate fishing diaries. He has stared at me from black and white photographs. He has haunted me and arrested my thoughts until I cannot escape the reality that I have drifted too far from a proper sporting path in recent years and that he has brought me back. He has made me remember the hills and the high lochs and I never again want to forget them. His name was Sidney Spencer. He died in a car accident in 1976 on the way to his beloved Lough Eske in magical Donegal. I did not know him; but I do now.

This book is a collection of Spencer's writing on the subject of lake fishing for trout, sea trout and salmon, an area of angling which obsessed the author and gave him such an intense insight into wild fish and wild places. In this desperately hard and cruel world where so much that is truly natural and wild has been lost, there is an ever-growing need in most of us to remember distant places we have loved, and better times. It is nostalgia, of course, but it is also a crying out of the heart in this modern darkness for something that we so need to recapture.

Spencer wrote for a different generation of fisherman.

Sportsmen today are better equipped in a technical sense, more numerous and mobile, and certainly more ruthless. My own peers might question the need to read and relearn accounts and events of someone who wrote, however beautifully, of fishing decades ago. But they would be wrong. Carbon fibre rods and Hi-D lines, fluorescent floss and pearlflash materials, heavily stocked rainbow trout fisheries and strident, quantitative sporting demands have, by and large, led us away from a philosophy and an outlook which are infinitely more valuable than those which prevail today.

There is greater dexterity today in the handling of rods and reels – and also of some gadgetry – than there has ever been, but this is but a little and without doubt the most easily acquired part of what is the accomplishment of a fisherman. The rest is knowledge of the world of fish and of the interplay of wind and weather, moving water, of the colours of earth and sky and of light, heat and cold. The more you can think like a fish the closer you are to being a 'cunning fisher'. To be so designated, in my beginning days in Scotland, was a great thing. It meant you had the known ability to catch fish in very difficult conditions, because by some strange alchemy you had the wild waterside in your blood, you had studied your fish in relation to the medium they lived in, you knew not only your flies but the way the fish liked them presented and the inelegance of your casting was no more than an eccentricity which the years would modify.

The dearly-loved sound was the seethe of waves on some far loch shore, the bubbling of the whaups and the deep croak of the raven. You could fish the evening rise, sleep the rain-filled night in the heather and rise to fish again in the dawn . . .

I hope the reader will approve my choice from Spencer's rich writing on lake fishing which has been collected in

Fishing the Wilder Shores. Much of his work covered method and technique, while the rest was anecdotal accounts of actual fishing days in the beautiful parts of the British Isles which infatuated him. This, really, was his great gift to us and is what I have mostly chosen.

A fishing life should be all about discovery. I remember so well, at home in the Weald of Kent, and then the prison of London, reading Spencer's *Salmon and Sea Trout in Wild Places* and *Newly from the Sea*. This was in the same period that I discovered big reservoirs like Grafham, the incredible beauty of Loch Maree and the wilderness lochs of the far north of Scotland. Although Spencer was usually writing about fisheries that were different from those I knew, the landscapes and nature of the fishing were the same. I did not know it then, but the images I saw in those pages and places were frighteningly transient. Who would have suspected, after all, that we would lose a fishery like Maree, possibly the finest sea-trout water that ever existed; or the idyllic Connemara and Mayo fishings, now almost devoid of migratory trout?

Today's fly fishermen have largely had the wild replaced with the artificial which, except for a few of the largest reservoir and lake fisheries, is a very poor state of affairs. We are living through this change. Yet by reading about the best of how it was not so long ago, it might affect us and give us some chance of protecting what remains and repairing what has been lost. And I believe that some of what Sidney Spencer described was the very best of the sport.

The author lived in Devon, where he fished a great deal on local rivers, reservoirs and lakes, though his heart lay farther north and west. By the late 1960s his visits to Scotland and the Hebrides were dwindling and his diary and writing were predominantly of fishing in Ireland.

County Donegal was paradise to him, and the last five or so years of his life were almost exclusively preoccupied by fishing on Lough Eske.

Those who knew him well speak of Spencer as a neat person generally, but in his fishing he was painstakingly precise. He enjoyed theorizing and often his fishing was largely experimentation and a means to explore the nature of fish, especially salmon and sea-trout. Even when he was being scientifically factual, however, one cannot escape the intense enthusiasm and sheer joy he experienced with all things to do with fishing.

In his extensive diaries, which run back to 1917 (though there are gaps lasting years), he records with the same enthusiasm episodes fishing for codling as he does when tench fishing on a quiet summer morning or catching small brownies from a hill lake in Wales. Pike particularly excited him through the 1930s and 1940s, though from some time in the 1950s onward he became entirely occupied by trout and salmon fishing.

Some of Spencer's evolution of thought and philosophy is less apparent in his books than in a study of his correspondence and diary. Peculiarly, he devoted almost half of his book *Ways of Fishing* (published in 1973) to clear water worm fishing, though apparently he had not utilized any form of bait fishing for two decades, despite having once been quite fond of fishing the upstream worm. I believe that he developed a dislike for taking trout and salmon on anything but fly. Trolling became ever more distasteful to him. He certainly became increasingly worried by the beginnings of what was to be the devastation of sea-trout populations over much of Britain. On this subject, on fish killing generally, and of our increasing dependence on artificial lakes, he was prophetic.

Though not designedly any sort of lament for days and ways that seem to be passing, these pages do contain, in lines written and unwritten, a plea for the dedication of new anglers to the preservation of all those things which have moulded and must always comprise an angling tradition. Without such a code, the finest sport in the world becomes merely a process of obtaining something to eat, give away or sell – preferably in large quantity. It is five hundred years since fishing was like that and the need behind the ancient fish-killing no longer exists.

Sidney Spencer was, I feel, first a passionate fisherman, interested in technicalities only in as much as they required precise attention so as to make him more effective in his sport, and in that they gave him a scientific appreciation of the results he obtained. Like so many truly great fishermen he developed some firm ideas about fly pattern and size for particular conditions. Then he must have possessed an artist's frame of mind when it came to his subjective interpretation of landscape and weather. He saw in these far more than their influence on the sport. The wild was certainly in his blood, and he knew it.

I have trodden the far-away paths of the otter and I have, for haunting, an unquenchable nostalgia for the wild. If it disturbs these pages I ask no pardon for an endeavour in honesty to preserve something greatly cherished by my kind of fisherman.

He was a loner to a certain extent, enjoying either his own company or that of close friends or quiet, thoughtful ghillies. He must have found heaven when, having dis-covered Lough Eske where he could invest all the time and energy of his latter fishing years, he also gained the long-term use of a caravan on its shores, where he could be alone. Here he lived and fished for long periods, an escapee of the 'new and strident world' which I think he feared.

Failure featured in Spencer's fishing, though he considered that a modicum of failure led ultimately to triumph.

Failure, which stimulates study and analysis has a great long-term virtue of its own. Too many older-time fishing books exuded repeated success and it can be wearisome. Failure is the challenge that will one day lead to celebration deserved but without conceit. A big bag on the day when the fish are 'on' is gratifying but no more – far preferable the time when a small or moderate total results from application of a lesson derived from previous defeat and directed at difficult fish or poor conditions.

But Spencer also made some glorious catches. He was fortunate to discover good fishing either close to his home or within his means to explore.

One suspects that he was not particularly wealthy, for there are a few pointed references here and there such as a diary log made at the end of 1966 which refers to him giving up his rod on the River Mole because of the cost. Rather, I believe he lived on the periphery of well-to-do society, happy to be there without the encumbrance of too many close relationships. But we shall probably never know for sure; Sidney Spencer, beyond his writing, remains an enigmatic personality.

He recorded the days when he made a spartan catch with scarcely less information than when the fish bag was swollen (he often referred to returning fish alive, especially brown trout and sea trout). It was the circumstance that fascinated him, not the result, though he certainly took a personal pride in taking big catches.

The author developed an empathy with the wild shore

which, to him, meant Lough Eske and the hinterland of County Donegal in Ireland's far north-west. There he lost his soul and there it will always rest. It will call out to other free spirits, to those who yearn for the last wild places where trout and salmon swim.

Jeremy Lucas
Weald of Kent, February 1991

The Point – A Hebridean Day

The wind blew a gale from the west and the west, in the location I describe means the open Atlantic. The sky at the western end of the loch always holds that infinity of emptiness which is an ocean sky and in the Hebrides, illuminated by the lights of the Isles, reminds you that you are, it seems, on the very edge of the world.

But the light that comes in most places with the west wind is a good fishing light, perhaps the best of all, and so it was when we hauled the boat from its heather cradle to the water's edge. Hopes ran as high as the waves on the sand – beautiful salmon-taking waves. It was a rough day on the loch and just as we had foreseen. For this day had been planned even more carefully than days on this loch have to be planned because of its remoteness away across six miles of mountainside broken with peat hags and endless ravines on the higher route, or very wet low ground on the other. Connected with the tide by a very short shallow river the loch gets, with any appreciable rain and a rise in the scores of small feeders, an immense run of sea trout and with them a few salmon.

Abounding in rocky points and clean pebble and sand shores it provides, I think, with its huge stock of medium weight fish, the finest sea trout fishing I know. It is uncommon to come away with less than eight or ten adult sea trout, which may, but do not always, run up to 5 or 6 pounds; apart from the finnock which are counted for record purposes but returned alive, as all finnock should be. And this, of course, in a very short fishing day since so much time is used in walking to and from the loch.

Thus, while this El Dorado glitters in one's thoughts over there on the rim of the western sea, one does have some regard, rather more careful than usual, because of its very remoteness, for conditions. An east or north-east wind day is useless because for one thing you must then fish over the best shore from shallow into deep and for another any north in the breeze will produce a nasty jabble against the best rocky point of all. To arrive after a gruelling trudge across terribly broken ground and find conditions bad is maddening, so one picks a day some time forward but decides to go only if at 10 a.m. summer time on that day, when the wind of the day has settled in, things look good.

The day I describe was such a day except that the plan was designed to make use of a watcher's report that some salmon had been seen to run the river a few days earlier and could reasonably be expected to have settled in one or other or maybe all of the three or four known lies. Combine this circumstance with a good west wind, a nice broken light and cloud carrying the odd shower or two and you may justifiably be happy in anticipation as I have indeed said we were. True, the wave was a great deal heavier than I like for sea trout, but I was after the salmon the watcher had seen and as for wind and wave, I had for ghillie the head keeper Angus, a man of exceptional physique and the best boat handler I know. On such a day, fishing over known lies of very limited extent, the man at the oars plays an equal part with the rod. That boat and rod are one instrument is a fact far too little appreciated by many anglers and some ghillies.

It was lunch time when, rod up and Yellow Torrish on the tail and Dusty Miller on the dropper, we pushed off after much pounding among the breaking waves. The Torrish normally does well on this loch and I had picked the Dusty for a dropper because I always think it fishes best in that position – and on this day, with plenty of sunshine, it should do well. The tail was a four (old scale) to steady the cast and the dropper a six, both larger than normal because of the big wave.

We drew first across a subsidiary bouldery point which often yields a fish but in spite of meticulously careful working, drew a blank. But we like a fish in the boat before going ashore for lunch and I personally find that sandwiches taste a lot better when you can look at a fish in the heather beside you as you sit under some peat bank out of the wind. So off we went across a narrow and very draughty inlet to try the main lie off the point which gives these notes their title. Here a thirty-foot bluff drops sheer into three or four feet of boulder-filled water – great round boulders these, gleaming golden under the marching waves rolling across the point. Perhaps an area twenty yards square forms the taking place and we edged down it foot by foot, Angus holding the boat head to wind, heaven knows how, while I fished, Hebridean fashion, off the stern. Further out and in deeper water than I expected, for fish often lie close-in under such conditions – the first fish made a little splashy rise like a trout and I left the fly where it was although I didn't think he had it. But he had, and I was in him – not a big fish as we saw when he jumped but a fresh one. We led him inch by inch it seemed up into that terrible wind and wave and presently put the net under a seven-and-a-half-pounder with the Dusty firmly where it should be, in the scissors.

'That boy's not by himself,' said Angus and I agreed.

These fish tend to stay in small companies for some time after entering fresh water and if a take is 'on them' you are likely to do well if you concentrate on a known lie. And so it proved for the next drift down produced another rise to the second cast – a very slowly-moving fish this time. I saw a light brown, almost golden, nose and the whole length of his back before he turned down and the line tightened. He came like a lamb out into deep water and disturbed the lie not at all. Then he suddenly realized something was wrong and gave us an exhibition of aerobatics at the end of a very long line – fortunately upwind, since I doubt whether the light cast would have withstood much of that wave pressure if drowned. Anyhow we had him aboard after seven or eight minutes and again the Dusty had done its job and again the fish was ideally hooked in the corner of his mouth. A nine-pounder this time.

So far so good. We decided to give the lie a wide berth and wallowed away downwind into the lee and thence into deep heather behind a quiet sandy beach for lunch. It was not a long break. If anything it was blowing harder than ever and a blue-black squall with cold fimbriated upper edges to its cloud-mass filled the western sky. I took the camera out of its waterproof bag and snapped the fish lying at the water's edge.

Back upwind of the lie we fished over the same ground again without response but a few feet inside the unfished area a little fish sailed out from between two sunken boulders and went quietly back with the fly. When I felt him we led him steadily out and after some deep boring and cast-thumping he came up and was netted – another victim of the Dusty and about six pounds. Whilst Angus held the boat head to wind out in deep water I cut the dropper out of the cast and re-tied dropper and fly. A cast is the better for re-tying – particularly at dropper and main cast knot, after it has handled a brace of fish. The squall was on us now and I fumbled at the blood knot with soft wet fingers while the cold rain poured off the brim of my fishing hat, the boat slammed down in the troughs and Angus grew impatient to be at them again. Obviously they were still 'on'. The light had gone and I wondered about changing the Dusty for a Black Doctor or a Thunder, but concluded that time was vital and the little pink-hackled fly certainly had been right so far.

We struck a blank patch this time down; from the centre of the lie down to the tail end of the jumble of boulders was either fish-less, or they had gone off, but well downwind from the normal taking area, when we were preparing to draw out and away again, I had a spectacular savage rise and to my surprise found the hook go home as firm as a rock. This fish would not be led – he simply was not having any of it. He went downwind as though the Norsemen who used to spear salmon in these waters were after him, and we were quickly into the backing. That raised no great problem of course and the boat was dropping down on him and I was recovering some line, when he suddenly veered off to the right, finishing close inshore on the shallows with dorsal fin and tail showing among breaking waves. He then came a bit deeper, went down still further and bored away up-wind. I now had twenty or thirty yards of sunk line and the wind of that accursed squall putting a frightening pressure on the belly from the rod-tip. I felt, for perhaps a minute, that something had to give but it didn't and out in the deep, where he had gone of his own accord, we played him out and netted him, Angus making the longest reach with the big net that I have ever seen, and getting very wet in the process – it really was a rough day. Another nine-pounder and another on the same fly.

I said that I would like to get another just to make five. What magic there was in five I do not know, but to be honest we both knew that it was finished and sure enough a further careful fishing of the entire area failed to produce any response. We baled the boat and considered. The other side of the loch four hundred yards away contained one lie at the mouth of an entering burn and two others off small undistinguished points of broken rocks. But these places could not be attained by direct passage in that weight of wind and wave and the only possibility seemed to be to take the boat upwind along our present shore, round in the lee of the head of the loch and drop down the other shore to fish the lies I have mentioned.

We found a little beach and I went ashore to lighten the boat while Angus applied his wonderful strength to driving the boat upwind, and I trudged through heather and bog to meet him in quiet water at the loch-head. Here is good sea trout ground but a change to smaller flies and lighter cast for the small waves of this quieter place served no purpose. As we drifted down the far shore, having fished across the head of the loch, we caught the wind again; the light cast came off and the cast of the morning was mounted again.

The river mouth where we confidently expected to find a fish was passed and the first of the points without sign of a rise. The squally weather had gone but the day was dark with none of the broken light which, with a lively wave, always flatters the fly and makes it easier to show it attractively, particularly in the dropper position.

However, at the second point and virtually the last of our unfished salmon lies, I had a deep quiet boil, instantly effaced by the rolling wave and the fifth fish was on, and pulling hard and steadily close to the boat. We took him out to safer water and there he surged about making no attempt at any sort of real run and keeping down. We both thought there was something odd about this fish. He just pulled hard without head-shaking, without showing and without head-down boring, and it went on like this until he came in the wall of a wave ten yards away and we both saw the best sea trout ever to come out of the loch – thick shouldered and golden of back and every spot on him showing up through the clear water. When we had him in the boat we found that we had to cut out the Dusty, so firmly was it fixed just forward of the scissors. 'This one will take some beating,' said Angus. 'He's a good six pounds.' He was later shown to be right.

And that was the end of that day. We fished down to the boat landing, even then reluctant to give up over an acre of possible salmon ground, but the day was done and we knew it. The water rolled sullenly under unbroken dark skies. An eagle, swinging in effortless spirals on the flank of the nearby hill, looked strangely light-coloured in that light.

The rollers carried us till we grounded with the bow on dry sand. Boat secured and fish washed and laid in the heather, I took another picture with misgivings about the light and presently we breasted the hill above the beach and with the wind in our backs, set out on our two-hour tramp to the lodge.

From the highest ridge we paused to look back at the loch – leaden silver against the western shore that separated it from the ocean gleam beyond. That, we said, and I still think, was a grand day! Five rises and five fish – four salmon and a big sea trout, and best of all, it went as we planned. You know, or if you don't you soon will, that in fishing this seldom happens.

Rough Weather

To some men, boat fishing in bad weather means the ultimate in discomfort, but it need not, and those of us who think little more of it than we do of the odd idyllic day have, each in our own way, solved the core of the problem – clothing. Boat fishing on reservoirs or lakes in the south is one thing, and on lochs in the north and west and in the offshore islands quite another. Rough wild fishing puts the maximum strain on every item of equipment, and if salmon and sea trout are your game you tend to find the best fishing in rough wild country and often when the weather is worst.

Gale-driven rain can be very searching and there are places where every third or fourth day will produce this sort of thing. Sit in a boat all day in such stuff and you cannot be comfortable, but you can be dry and warm. Indeed, unless you are, you cannot fish with any sort of concentration and the whole exercise becomes some kind of penance. Salmon and sea trout together or separately are found in all manner of lakes – from the big ones in the glens to small pools in the high headwaters of river systems. Very big lochs breed their own brand of weather and little ones are subject to weather engendered by the surrounding terrain. The one probably suffers from sheer sweep of wind over a long expanse of water – the other maybe from location among mountains that funnel wind and produce appalling squalls. I know two good sea trout lochs squeezed between high precipitous hills; both are all but unfishable and on one of them I have seen solid masses of water weighing many tons picked up off the wave-tops and flung high in the air. These are extreme cases, of course, and fortunately bear little relation to normal fishing conditions.

The point, however, is that to take advantage of the finest in the salmon and sea trout world one must be prepared for the worst weather that the best lochs can produce. Add to this the fact that salmon often do best on wild days and you want to be out if it is humanly possible. I can never quite make up my mind whether bank or boat fishing presents the greater problem in heavy rain. On the bank you have the need for mobility so that your outfit must be light in weight; in the boat you may literally sit in water and rain is driven at you from all directions as the boat changes position; weight doesn't matter but water-proofness does and is vital. On the bank you move about and keeping warm is not so very difficult – in the boat it is very different.

Most important is a means of preventing that cold trickle down the back of the neck and the general damp-ness in that region. Take a rough towel of ordinary size – not one of those foolish little hand towels, nor a bath towel – and cut it end-to-end in six-inch wide strips. Have the cut edges hemmed and you have three or four towel-ling scarves which will protect neck and chest and mop up any wet which gets between hat and collar. I can think of no other single article which has so contributed to my comfort in the boat, simple as it is.

Unlike some anglers I have met, I do not consider that getting wet or stiffened by cold is any part of fishing. It is quite unnecessary and a proper kit will avoid it even in the worst of wild wet days in the boat. Also – another simple thing – have your boat trousers fitted with fixed braces rather than belt or draw-cord. Something depends on the wearer's figure of course, but these trousers which fasten at the waist usually slip down – the resulting duck-like waddle when you go ashore will assuredly amuse the ghillie and rob you of any natural dignity you may otherwise exhibit!

From weatherproofness to general comfort in the boat is a ready transition and cushions at once come to mind. Most of them are good in dry weather and just so much spongy soggy lumber in wet. If, as is usual, they are foam rubber or some form of synthetic foam of open cell structure they soak up water even when fitted with supposedly waterproof covers because on a really wet day the water finds its way in through the seams of the cover. If you can get a slab of heavy cellular rubber seating used for upholstery purposes and cover this with some carefully-seamed and completely waterproof material, you have a reasonable compromise but I know of nothing one hundred per cent satisfactory when boat seats are streaming water, unless it is the ghillie's potato sack stuffed with straw! A really wet seat can be very unpleasant and I have obviated it with the combination of three-quarter-length coat; double-seated trousers and heavy rubber cushion.

Life is a great deal easier in boats, whatever the weather, if some simple discipline in small things is observed by both fisherman and ghillie and some of the latter need instruction by example, or in obdurate cases, by straight expression of wish. I dislike loose gear about the boat – fly boxes, scissors, the baler, the net and the like and I keep my fishing bag under the stern seat if I am alone and fishing from there, or right up in the bow if I am bowrod, and drop each item back in the bag after use. The net goes in front of the ghillie on his right. In very wet weather I put fly boxes, spare reel, the camera, and binoculars in a big polythene bag inside the fishing bag proper and knot the bag neck to keep out wet. The lunch bag is stowed always in the bow under an old waterproof, or otherwise protected. Incidentally, while all good ghillies will bale the boat dry before you leave the landing, some do not. An inch or two of water will not bother you in your rubbers but it can and often does soak bags stored on the floor boards. Of course, boats can be dry when you start and, leaking like baskets, flood everything in the course of a day. I find that boats, especially in Ireland, have gone through several phases. Years ago there were some incredibly decrepit craft, going to pieces from age or neglect or both, and rotten and leaking. Then there was an intermediate stage when many of these ancients were replaced and Irish boats generally were better-conditioned. Of recent years, with prices for new boats soaring, I seem to detect a renewed decline in boat condition. In the 'thirties, one could buy a good larch boat in Ireland for about a pound a foot of length. It is very different now.★

Few boats actually suit one rod – they drift better and make life easier for the ghillie with a fisherman of rather over-average weight in the bow. A single rod can sometimes trim a boat inclined to twist on the drift by moving out of the stern seat on to a board closer amidships. I look for slow steady drifting in a boat, which means one with a good 'grip' – one that does not slide to leeward. Stability is also vital. I never stand up to fish but I frequently stand

★ Editor's note: In the last decade, of course, we have had to get used to glass fibre boats, especially on Scottish lochs. In Ireland the boats on many loughs have actually been replaced by excellent new wooden boats.

in the final stages of playing a fish because I like to see how deep the fish is and what he is doing when he comes close to the boat. For this you need a stable steady boat that will not roll as she rises and falls and lurches in a big wave. With feet braced apart, you should be able to balance with confidence and attend to the doings of your fish.

Here boat tidiness comes in again. The ghillie must know exactly where to put his hand on net and priest. I have seen many a chance of netting missed because the ghillie had to twist around in his seat to get the net from under painter and other gear in the bow. In really rough conditions he should be able to keep at his oars until the last moment, shipping oars and picking up net almost in one swift movement as a passing chance presents itself. If the priest is at hand the fish can be killed quickly and left in the net for unhooking later while the ghillie, back at his oars, regains lost ground. Before we leave drifting boats, there is one more thing – elementary – but often ignored. If wind and wave are such that the boat drifts quickly in the latter stages of playing your fish, keep him on the windward side where he is infinitely safer. Do not let the ghillie keep him so by moving the boat; in so doing you change or are likely to change the angle of the hold. Do it by persuasion with the rod. If your fish plays downwind and close to the boat, you may go over him, so steer him back to windward. But beware of too hard a hold if he runs upwind in a big wave because the drifting boat is pulling at him as well as the strain you yourself exert via the rod. It is this situation that produces the scene all too familiar – the angler playing a fish far to windward of the boat and slowly losing line from a rod pulled down almost parallel with the water. This rod angle, always bad, in these circumstances can be disastrous because maximum strain is on the tackle and the rod absorbs little or none of the pull. The oldest maxim in fishing, 'keep the rod up', can never lose its soundness but is often forgotten.

From bad weather clothing to boat tidiness, boat behaviour, and tactics in handling fish is, I think, if wide ranging and some digression at least appropriate to the context of wild weather fishing on lochs. Most of the art of extracting the best out of rough fishing conditions lies in small things which coalesce in a craft belonging to a very keen band who are on the loch and getting fish when the fine-weather men are in the hotel bar waiting for the wind to drop. No point, of course, in going out if you do not enjoy it.

I like rough days though I dislike a persistent downpour which softens hand and tackle, reduces cigarettes to pulp, and sometimes puts fish off. But I would like a fiver for every 'bad' day I have fished and got my fish before lunch, sat under a gorse bush or ashore on some inlet, huddled over lunch in the shelter of some undercut peat bank or overhanging rock. There are the birds to watch and there are worse sounds, to me, than the chuck-chuck of waves under the stern of the drawn-up boat. Speaking of beached boats there are some features of the care of gear – some of the small things I spoke of – that are worth a thought whenever you go ashore leaving rods and tackle in the boat. When I have finished for the day I always put rods safely away and dry them first and pull line off the reels before I do anything else and neither my ghillie nor I get our day's-end dram until this duty is discharged. But shorter absences from the boat often see the rods left there and it is then that damage is done, especially on a rough day. I find that ghillies very properly take pains to see that the boat is secure and beyond risk of damage, but they are often curiously blind about rods. Admittedly the rods are the fisherman's concern but some fishermen, normally careful of their rods, are careless of them in the boat.

When a boat is beached temporarily she will be drawn up far enough to ensure that she does not float off but not so far up that it will be difficult to push off again, and in rough weather the stern will bump. If the rods are put in the bow they can be damaged when you clamber ashore and if they are put in the stern, as happens in ninety per cent of cases, they will bob and rattle as the waves nudge the boat stern, and so damage their varnish. Again, when boats are secured at a jetty or pier, rods are often left projecting over the stern and are damaged, if not broken, by the next careless boat that ties up nearby.

In either situation rods should be brought inside the boat and laid from bow to stern along the thwarts so that the butt and the top rings are inside the gunwales. They are perfectly safe, even in a bouncing boat on a badly-exposed beach, provided the oars are prevented from rolling or sliding either by jamming under thwarts or by being laid blades flat on say, stern seat, along the thwarts. If you think that even these precautions are not enough, take the rods ashore and prop them somewhere in sight at a forty-five-degree angle. So placed they will neither be trodden on nor blown over.

March Day

The wind, like the empty sky to the north, had the quality of hard blue steel. It came cruelly over the snow encrusted skyline and down the mountain to the lake to raise hard blue waves on the shallows by the inflowing river. The light was as hard as the wind and down at the boat landing I could see every grain of sand, every dead leaf and every tuft of moss in five feet of water with the unnatural clarity peculiar to this and certain other qualities of light. No lough and few rivers will ever fish when you can see clearly so deep down.

Some waters are, of course, always clear but there are degrees in the characteristic – the bad one is always marked by an odd dead look difficult to describe but instantly recognizable if you have seen it before and associated it – beyond dispute – with utter unresponse in the fish. The rule is good for salmon, sea trout and trout and for coarse fish – especially pike. On such days I have learnt, by devastating but interesting experience, to expect little but I nevertheless try to fish, confident in my own ability to offset the poor conditions. It is a fine conceit but any other attitude of mind will keep one too often away from the water. So, for my part, I indulge the fancy and come back, occasionally, with the unexpected fish.

I looked at the lough this March day with a growing

conviction that no salmon would come to the fly on such
a day so early in the season.

You see, I wanted a fish very much for a special occasion
and there were fresh fish in the lake in, it was believed,
moderate numbers. If the water was not *too* cold who
knows, we might get one on the fly – that 'might' that
keeps us fishing on the bad days! I put a hand overside as
we pulled away from the landing and was thankful to
withdraw it pretty smartly – the trailed thermometer
showed a bare 36°F. The mountain bedrock was cold after
a hard winter and the daily melt water from the snow-
filled gullies gained little in temperature on its way down
to the lake. My mind's eye pictured fresh salmon sullen in
the cold twenty-foot deeps off the river sand's edge which
was my fishing ground – but we could conceivably get a
mild hour or so at midday of sun time.

Meanwhile wind direction dictated that we must begin
inshore and so fish from shallow into deep if we followed
a conventional drift pattern – and I never like this. So we
butted our way down the western shore: in the stern and
facing the wind I was glad of a thick neck towel – this
particular wind was a sharp finder of spaces between coat
buttons.

We presently lay to in the north-western corner of the
fishing area with two choices before us, one a pull inshore
on the north beach and work straight out with wind and
wave run in a series of short drifts or, two, not to drift at
all but to pull along the shore fishing on the move –
beginning close inshore and with each successive quarter
mile passage fishing a strip further out. Wise choice now
might mean a fish, the wrong one a blank. The first
method would spoil a great deal of water and involve the
fishing from shallow to deep which, as I have said, is bad
technique – the second would cover all the water more

slowly and with a less marked outward clearing effect of possible shallow lying fish. So that was how it was to be.

Fly choice was another question almost as difficult and the problem mainly one of size. Water so clear demanded a seven or even an eight but its temperature and the early season called aloud for a six or even a four – at all events something that on a sinking line would swim low down and a little nearer those torpid salmon. I hadn't much faith in the dropper but a bright fly might bring a fish up and a Silver Doctor seemed to fill the bill – size a six. On the tail went a four Golden Olive – its heavy iron and quickly sodden wool body designed to take it deeper.

The first traverse of the shallow water produced a thin brown trout of about two pounds which should have been three – the trout are still unfed and keltish in March in that place. The return progress brought us a little nearer sensible fishing depth but was utterly blank. Back in our NW corner I told James to put the boat's nose on the shingle while we had a cup of coffee. The wind swooped round the hill shoulder behind us and blackened the water momentarily on top of the main wave. Failure was blowing in that wind.

The next two crossings of the fishing area should cover the best of the water – water eight to ten feet out over the edge of the river delta where salmon lay thickly and in May with warmer water and favourable winds would rise freely. There wouldn't be many fish there now but assuredly there were some and it was about noon by the sun. I fished it thoroughly, slowly and deep – James working the boat at matching speed. Seventy or eighty yards out I had a sharp firm take by a fish that obviously meant to have the fly. Two or three short snatches followed and he went off about thirty yards and then came up circling the boat close under the surface. A pallid gleam presently confirmed that we had a kelt very quickly netted and released. There is always doubt for the first three or four minutes because some kelts spawned not far from the lake are extraordinarily strong for their condition and a well-mended one will actually provide a rather better fight than many a tired fresh fish. I have never believed in the proposition that there is a wide difference between the silver of a fresh fish and the chrome of a kelt but there *is* an elusive difference – difficult to define. I would say, I think, that the fresh fish has the underlying glow of condition which gives it colour as well as brightness and very often this can be seen while the fish is in play. Other features are apparent once the fish is in the hand, of course, and there are also differences in the form of activity immediately after the hook goes home. The convulsive arc-ing of the body which in a fresh fish has deliberation and power becomes wriggly when the fish is a kelt.

The remainder of that drift produced a few small thin brownies and three attempts by one very obvious kelt to grab the tripping dropper, here fishing very nicely in the bigger offshore wave. The sun shone on glinting blue water – much too blue I thought because blue light conditions which come from a cloudless highly coloured sky are seldom good on this lough – nor for that matter, on most others. And, to make matters worse, the taking time – or what should have been the taking time – was passing. The final drift would cover the best of the water.

I could not shake off the strong impression of lifelessness that the look of the water conveyed to me – lifelessness that is, in terms of fresh fish. This was bad and I knew it but we began the last drift: I fished it with meticulous care, and as slowly as I felt the conditions demanded. At its termination the boat was in position to drift broadside down a very good stony shore, almost but not quite as productive as the river sands and I decided to fish about two hundred yards of it downwind, in fact, until it ended at a shallow shingle point itself a good lie.

This shore is a favourite of mine. It possesses all the features which make good holding ground. Gently shelving from a sandy turfy margin backed by thickets of myrtle at the foot of a steep hillside, the water is five feet deep at twenty feet from shore, the bottom of clean waterworn stones in a matrix of sand and fine gravel. Moreover, there are in its length three wave-demolished wall-ends which in due season hold fish and the final point has given me salmon often enough for me to have infinite faith in it.

About half way along this most promising shore then I saw, two cast lengths ahead, a small break in the water which looked remarkably like the mark of a fish moving 'to himself'. James hadn't seen it but I could cover it easily in a few moments and did so without result. But there did appear – literally from nowhere, in the lane between boat's bow and shore a very surprised looking merganser. And as it vanished below I saw again the little water break that *could* have been a fish. Still – on the credit side, an unusually close look at a shy bird, seldom so tolerant of near approach.

When we sheered out to pass the shallow sunken spit of shingle off the point I knew we were beaten and the day had proved itself to be what it had looked from its beginning – a bad one for the fly. It was three o'clock and the wind as hard and cold as ever. If there had been any softening in the middle of the day we hadn't noticed it and it hadn't affected the move of those cold-inhibited salmon. James unclamped frozen hands from the oars, I reeled up and we drifted idly for a spell. The vision I had been cherishing of the first fish of the season presented with its garnishing of lemon and cucumber for my guests at tomorrow's dinner party was fading . . . in truth had faded.

There remained one faint hope. We were nearly a mile from home and the trolled Toby might attract a fish on the way. Though I had brought the spinning rod I hesitated now that it had come to what is known in today's vernacular as the crunch. My own distaste of trolling I discounted but I could not ignore what I disliked even more – the very obvious chance of hooking one of the clearly fairly numerous kelts and of tearing its mouth with the triangle of the Toby. A kelt hooked on fly and carefully freed so that it does not bleed is one thing – a similar fish on a spinning bait whatever the care is quite another. I was not, however, worried about spoiling fly water – we were by now far outside that and would not cover it on the way to the boat landing – besides – I really did want that fish rather badly.

It is a commentary on my dislike of trolling that I hesitated so long and that when I did put the bait overside I did so with a faint self-contempt. Here I was, a dedicated fly man – publicly scorning the lowly and skill-deficient ways of taking a fish – doing that very thing. Maybe the very truth of my weakness will induce your charity.

The better offshore wind had much more drive out here and the wave crests were broken: we were in the zone where the white horses first became visible – I knew that looking upwind from the south end of the lough into the lee sides of the rollers it must look unfishable but that we could lurch our way home across wind and wave. I knew, moreover, that this same lurch would put on the bait without effort on my part the enticing leap and dive that otherwise only a 'worked' troll could have.

Forty-five yards of line went out yard by yard – James

pulled as steadily as the boat's motion would let him while I clamped a frozen hand round the multiplier. While the line was taut between plunges of the boat I could feel the throb of the Toby in the deep far astern. To get it down I had put a smallish Hillman lead on the upper eye of the top swivel.

We passed forty yards outside the seaward end of a well-known sunken reef and here came the savage pull that almost took the rod from my hand. The fish went back the way we had come and had a great deal of line before James could wear the boat round working slowly upwind.

We presently had the fish directly below us and there I played him – James maintaining our position lest, as he said, we should be blown 'to hell and gone' down the lough. The fish, it soon became evident, was not the kelt that I dreaded – here was no short-lived activity, no soft play. This was a hard fresh fish as a run and a spray scattering jump proved. I played him rather gently but without one inch of slack – and particularly so when he came towards the boat, diving and twisting and wrenching against the short stiff rod. Dangerous moments these, and I did want that fish!

James seemed to stow the oars and extend the net in one smooth movement and we had him – about twelve pounds, fresh and clear and hard and shining. There were no anglers among tomorrow's guests and I shouldn't be asked how I got him. I hooked up the Toby and stowed the rod away. We had drifted far downwind even in that short time and now we had a fish in the boat, we both shook with cold and relieved tension: I tried to light a cigarette and gave it up until we had the shelter of the boathouse.

Frown at my doings if you will but having read this far I think that your feelings will be as mixed as were mine – walking up from the landing with that first fish of the season – so badly wanted.

After the Storm

The storm had blown itself out. Gone was dark racing wrack from overhead and the mountains were clear of cloud and soft of outline. The tortured woods were all but still and the reed-beds erect again. The air was new and fresh and the rain had gone – a high lake and the sound of rushing rivers remained. At the lough head a curtain of white water had spread across a great smooth rock face and fell two hundred feet to be lost in a rickle of broken rock whence issued the river proper.

There was a fishing breeze and no more, but it was westerly and that source together with the life and fresh-ness of its air gave me high hopes.

The lough, on the other hand, was far too high and far up into the trees behind the foreshores; some low-lying grassy islets had disappeared. We had three feet too much water and the entering river draining some agricultural land in its lower reaches, surged in a brown swirling flood far out into the lake. Rafts of dead vegetation, sticks, fencing posts and all the riverside junk of a twenty mile course, to say nothing of Barney Mulreany's old pig shed, twisted and gyrated on the surface.

One thing was certain – only a limited area of the river entry would be clean enough to be fishable at least as far as salmon were concerned, but sea trout should be feeding on the fringes of the current in the newly-flooded grassy bays and perhaps on the shallow bar across the river mouth.

Such a day takes a great deal of appraisal and there had been much weighing of pros and cons on this day in advance of a decision to fish. Tomorrow with a lower lake would be infinitely better but would it blow too hard again – and would the wind stay in the west? – if it went sou-west it would rain again and with the mountains saturated as they were, any rain would run off at once and feed the lake so that it would hold its present excessive height. But the lake never fishes when it is high and no local will trouble to try. I am not a local and I don't like the word 'never' in fishing. Also, in the midst of our deliberations, I had remembered that I had once had three salmon when the lake was high up among the gorse. So, in the end, the boat was hauled down from her secure berth high among the trees and away we went.

I will just admit – and then get on with my story – that I was still assailed by doubt and shuffling a bit in my seat as Michael pulled away from the home bay and headed for the fishing ground.

Arrived there we paused at the upward end of a long drift that would take us across the river mouth and the best of the ground – gravelly and boulder-strewn water of four to eight feet in normal conditions and now carrying almost double that depth. Even from a couple of hundred yards away the line of the main current was sharply demarcated but we were in clear amber water and any fish with a mind to look could see the fly. Michael placed the boat close inshore. Looking around I could see sun-bleached stones covered for the first time in weeks. I don't think salmon move inshore in a lake with rising water: they lack the feeding impulse that pulls sea trout in and unless there is a strong inshore wind they tend in my experience to stay where they are – but I do believe strongly in the inclination of salmon to move downwind in any considerable blow (hence my reference to an inshore breeze).

We debated mildly about where the fish might be while the boat travelled fifty yards and then without bidding from me Michael pulled offshore until we were almost but not quite on our normal line of drift with, now, about eight feet of water under the keel. I was fishing a No. 7 Silver Grey, on the dropper because I thought it suited the light and a No. 6 Fiery Brown on the tail as a concession to the dirty water which we should presently be working. The cast was 8 lb. nylon. A sea trout of something over a pound snatched the Silver Grey and was duly netted as we approached the line where clear water ended and the muddy current began. 'Here,' I said to Michael, 'is where the fish should be,' and was about to tell him of similar circumstances on another day and another lough, when a fish rose beautifully to me – turned away with the current and was firmly on. We led him after a short run, away from the taking place and into deeper water. After following like a lamb he suddenly became active in a peculiar way – snatching and jigging and when held hard gyrating and twisting and making short turns with body all but doubled. I now knew I had a grilse for these quick turns are typical and grilse it was – fresh and about six pounds. He looked good in the boat – foundation for what might be a good day: Michael looked happy – we had been right to come out after all.

The west wind blew steadily and we worked slowly across it and along the edge of the current. Conflicting wave drive and flow of current produced a confused jabble in which a fly cannot be made to work properly and I was not surprised that we moved nothing better than smallish brownies in the disturbed water. There might be sea trout, however, further out in the lake where the weight of flow eased a little and we let the boat go with the pull of moving water – to no avail – too much floating rubbish. In fact this kind of fishing is a waste of time when the water is so laden with debris that the fly travels barely a foot or so before hooking in a load of leaves, bents, twigs and whatnot. It is not the inconvenience of having to flick this stuff off the hook – and how it will sometimes stick! – that matters but the fact that fish will not stay – much less take – in water carrying gill-clogging flood debris in suspension at all levels.

We had fished the upwind fringe of the muddy current and we had tried – I can't say fished – the stream itself: there remained the greater portion of the fishing area which with the wind westerly lay downwind of the river and its trashy burden. So we pulled across the current and then, as expected, found muddy water extending as far as we could see downwind. It had a depressing fishless air about it when I began to fish, rather slowly and deep: four hooded crows sitting in a cluster of villainy on an ash sapling by the shore let loose a chorus of derisive croaks. I couldn't see the Silver Grey an inch under the surface and I replaced it with a Keating Killer of the same size but much more prominent in the murky water.

In that sweet breeze the boat drifted at very good fishing speed over some of the best salmon ground in the lough: time of day was the best for that place and season – about an hour after noon by the sun. And in a quarter of a mile of steady fishing we didn't move a fin. We turned back to clear water beyond the river and again I fished the wavering junction of clean and muddy water with scrupulous care, putting the flies into the swirl of the current and working towards the boat so that the flies appeared out of the murk into sparkle and clarity. In theory it seemed good – and I have known it work well – but this day it did not and I really think we had too much depth – in short, the lough really was too high – the grilse was a fluke.

There remained one possibility of further sport. In the left or downwind side of the river mouth as we looked at it from the boat offshore was a sandy bay with low grassy shores fringed by scrub. The water was now over the grass and into the aforesaid scrub but the bay was on the edge of, yet completely out of the river current. It was of course thoroughly muddied but it was also, so I reasoned, the settling place for much of the ground feed coming off the fields and down the river. We might find feeding sea trout there. We did – they were close in on the grass.

The first to come to the Keating was a 2½ pounder as fat as butter until he was tapped on the head when he disgorged a mass of slugs, worms, woodlice and so forth. Three casts later another and better fish took with the jolting take of a sea trout feeding hard and was in turn duly netted – a three pounder this time and much less distended. Two fish of about a pound came to hand before the bay was covered. We had worked the shore from the river to the eastern margin of the bay and now Michael pulled slowly back while I cast a long run to swing, curving, behind the boat and be cast again. That failed to bring anything up and back at the river again I was torn between another drift and the feeling that with five sea trout and a grilse in the boat we had had our share in poor conditions.

In the end I chose to fish half a dozen casts in a little corner which we had not yet touched. It lay just where current ceased to come into the bay but so close inshore that my first cast alighted between two gnarled gorse stems. The flies came clear and I cast again along the current edge. And a salmon came very slowly and quietly up, turned across and into the current and was on. He had taken the Fiery Brown on the tail and when he shot through the current and I held him firmly on a fixed length of line to lead him, the dropper came up with a plume of dead grass on it. Next time it might be a branch or a length of fencing and the sooner we had that fish the better. He made one more longish run but by then we had worked him into clear water, where there was no scrap, floating or otherwise.

He was a slightly red cock fish of 11 lbs. and after Michael had washed the net and his hands and had his smoke, we turned homeward – day ended.

It contained some lessons, that day. Its events don't in the least invalidate my certain knowledge that high water does not suit that lough nor many others. But it does prove that one unfavourable condition may not be enough to offset the effect of good features of the day – i.e. wind, temperature, clear air and light. Above all it does indicate, I think, the value of appreciation of the ways of the fish and their probable behaviour in a given condition. I give myself credit for the grilse and the feeding sea trout because I expected to find them where I did – the taking salmon in that thick mud at the river proves only that after all these years I can be frightfully wrong about what is likely!

Weather Change

It began with a shift of wind. Before then the day had been just another of light breeze from a not very favourable quarter – the north-west to be precise. That source of wind didn't suit the south-eastern fishing ground because of the three-mile run of waves it provided there once it had what I call salmon-fishing strength. Rough lively waves are one thing but big rollers lurching too steeply for a drifting boat are quite another.

So, with the north-west wind despite its no more than medium weight making the southern area of the lake a doubtful proposition we had gone, James and I, to the north end which we preferred anyhow given a suitable breeze. Salmon were inclined to be dour but a north-west driven ripple would suit the sea trout admirably and I looked for a good day's fishing in fair, if not first-class conditions.

I was wrong. That wind did nothing for us. It was inclined to fluctuate from pleasant steadiness to near squalls but that was hardly enough in itself to account for total non-response in the sea trout. We covered ground where we knew sea trout were present in newly-arrived shoals and we saw a few small brown trout. I thought that the time was wrong – as it so often is with sea trout – and that there would be a rise sometime before one o'clock sun time. The light was fairly good through broken cloud and the air was warm. We idled in the boat watching the sandpipers on the shingle and testing our skill to call the curlew flighting overhead. They are hard to deceive but you can make a bird swing round and down just once – and only once.

Theoretically we should have been fishing intently because it had come to eleven-thirty and we had not so much as a scale in the boat. We had been wasting time and then suddenly without warning it was calm. On our lough and indeed on most that I know, a calm will be followed by a change of wind, beginning with a few puffs from any and every direction and followed by a settling in from one of them. I said as much to James who kept studying the horizon and was concerned mainly lest it should back and blow too freshly from the south – indicating a hard pull home.

But it did not come from the south – it came down due north from the mountain – a real cold fresh breeze and in our situation, blowing directly offshore. Worse still it was gusty, scuttering black patches across the lough, and aloft it was filling in with uniform dark cloud everywhere. I didn't like it one little bit because with us it can blow really hard from the north. And I do not like fishing, as we were now forced to do, from shallow into deep – whatever the wind's source.

I have been fishing for sea trout a very long time indeed and they still surprise me. They surprised me now because in that cold gusty wind and very poor light, they began to rise. They didn't take well but they did rise. At one time to the Donegal Blue and a small Silver Doctor, I seemed to be rising fish to every cast that I could fish out between gusts. I think that in half an hour or thereabouts I must have risen thirty fish. A few were obvious finnock but the majority were fish of one to one-and-a-half pounds; and when they ceased to make swirls at the fly we had ten of them. Neither gust nor chill seemed to put them off while the general move was on them. I have seldom seen less promising looking water. It was broken into little ragged heaps without concerted movement, tortured into minia-ture maelstroms of gust-blackened waves and above all carrying that abomination of all water-surface conditions, a wave on top of the wave. If I had not seen it I would not have believed that fish would come to the fly. Nor would James, and I have a feeling that lesson will keep coming to mind.

When we pulled in to the shore for lunch the wind had increased markedly and the body of the lough was break-ing into white horses everywhere.

Under a rowan bush on the turf bank behind a little sandy beach we were comfortable enough and indeed must have so looked because we were presently joined by another boat – angler and ghillie both of our acquaintance. They had had a long rough pull up the lough and were glad to shelter. The fish in our boat astonished them: they had tested some of the best points along the shore wholly without result. Clearly our take was local. We agreed that there appeared little hope for the remainder of the day. If anything the wind was strengthening and it looked like building into one of those days of the big rolling combers that lift the silt on the shallower fishing grounds and make much water useless until some hours after both wind and silt go down again.

We stayed ashore for some time. Normally we forget lunch until we are sure that the usual midday taking time is over and then take our time over it. But we don't normally waste good fishing time: today was different for, to be truthful, I didn't know where to go. The only water sheltered from the blustering north wind and on the way to our home landing was a weedy bay full of hungry little brownies and little else so that further fishing for anything worthwhile appeared non-existent. A boat could no longer be held in position where we had found our sea trout so that all that was left seemed to be a straight run home.

Even that defeatist course held some problems because if the lough lapping our beach at the head of this wind was rough, what would it be like at our home landing where the wave would have had two miles of open water in which to build up? Even at that distance we could see flickering fountains of white spray bursting on the southern shore rocks and we knew that no boat could live in that sea. Unless you fish big lakes you can have no vision of the kind of roughness that can develop from mountain-derived winds of any strength.

But plan for the return there had to be and it could take one form only. There was, about three-quarters of a mile downwind from us, a long low point jutting athwart the wind and at its landward end a great sandy shallow thickly grown with reeds. If we could attain that place we could safely allow the boat to be driven or to be washed ashore through the sheltering reeds, and thence walk home knowing the boat to be high and dry and beyond harm on the beach behind the aforesaid reeds.

This plan had two defects in the shape of two hazards. At one point on the route the wind, now freshened to something like a full gale, was funnelled between a high rocky, timbered island and the shore, and here in the shallow channel there would be a steep boat-swamping wave. Beyond that lay four hundred yards of open water which we must cross to reach the reeds. The wind would be dead astern all the way. I said that our home-going plan could take but one form but we did very briefly consider the one alternative which was to leave the boat where she was and walk from there. This would require the tortuous traverse of over a mile of densely-wooded hillside before we could reach open ground. Fresh and alert and unburdened one can, in fact, negotiate those woods but in a lifetime of scrambling I have never known such a jungle – its floor littered with broken rock, gnarled roots and fallen trees, hanging lichen swamping the lower branches of living timber – true primeval forest. Today with rods and miscellaneous gear to carry, its passage would be both exhausting and temper fraying.

If this is a long recital with precious little fishing to enliven it I can only plead that days like this will occur as a part of fishing and that however well you know your lough and your local weather, you cannot anticipate every wind shift and you must occasionally be 'caught'.

The other boat, talking vaguely of waiting for wind drop, wished us luck as we pushed off and even went so far as to say 'Ye'll get yer salmon on the way home!' We thanked them, of course and we parted with no shadow of hope. But I did take off the sea trout cast and replace it with one of 8-pound nylon carrying two sixes – one a Dunkeld and the other a Sweep: as we left the shore I put out about fifteen or twenty yards of line and allowed it to trail astern. In a rough wave salmon will often take a trailed fly when they won't look at one cast to them and worked. We would pass a very small area of good salmon ground on our way.

Conditions in the channel between island and shore when we reached it, were on the borderline between what is passable and what is so bad that only a fool would try it. So great was the pressure of wind and wave however that we had no choice: we were committed and could not turn inshore since any single wave on quarter or beam would have swamped us. James dug his oars in and held on and we swooped and soared onwards like any speed-boat. The wind was curling the wave tops and whipping them off. I sat on the floor and baled the water swilling over the boards, but we caught less wind this way and we took only spray and no solid water.

When we were rather more than halfway through, I hooked a fish. As a fact I had nothing to do with it. I had secured the butt of the rod at a slight diagonal, reel handles uppermost and had all but forgotten it when the reel screamed and went on screaming. Backing was partly gone when I got the rod up to a sensible angle and clamped a finger on the line. And there I sat in an inch or two of dirty water holding the rod butt nearly vertically and literally dragging that fish with us. James was helpless and could only cling to his oars and try to slow us down while I waited for the break. I thought it had come when for a second or two the pressure eased completely. But it came on again with a sudden snatch as we sailed on. Generally speaking, that fish came quietly – surging along behind us and now and then showing in the wall of a following wave.

Now there was a place where the channel splayed into completely open water, on our left and on our right, into an indentation hardly deep enough to be called a bay on the main shore and here the rough water eased down a little to become a heavy surge – uncomfortable but relatively quiet. A touch on one oar and we shot into the 'shelter' of this semblance of a bay. Twenty yards more and we were close inshore where tall mixed timber stood as a partial wind break at the water's edge on a steep beach of broken rock. In terms of being pulled by the head that fish had had a rough time, but in terms of resistance he had come like a lamb for something like a hundred and fifty yards – and now he woke up. If, a few moments earlier, he had used all the tricks he now employed, we should never have got him so far. He went straight down, smacking the cast hard. Water was very deep here and looked safe enough until you looked closely, when you saw the maze of fallen larch timber with laddered branches that cluttered the bouldery bottom sliding steeply into the gloom of great depths. It was a horrible place in which to play a fish and James and I looked at each other in something like amazement when, at last, we had a very fresh-looking ten pounder in the boat.

There were two separate and distinct hook tears in the mouth so that I had come very near to losing him before that snatch had signalled a fresh grip of the hook. For what it was worth he had taken the Sweep but I thought then, and still think that the impulse to take came from the speed of the fly, the lure of a darting shape passing at high speed and not from its pattern.

We sat in the rocking boat close under the trees for a while, studying the look of our final hazard, the open gale-torn stretch between us and our designated haven behind the reeds. This stage was twice as long as the passage through the island channel which we had weathered very well, but in the open the waves were longer crest to crest and less broken. I cannot say that we made the crossing, when we did finally leave shelter, with any comfort, either mental or physical: I am quite sure that boat had never travelled so fast in her history but I was very wet from sitting in sloshing water when her nose drove into the reeds. Successive surges, damped down by the forest of stems but still full of drive, carried us shorewards until we grounded in a few inches of water over firm sand.

We emptied the boat of all her movable gear, rods, sodden fishing bag, lunch bag and the fish and hauled her high above flood marks, there to lash her to a tree with the long nylon painter I carry for this purpose. A short painter is always an abomination, but a long one can be a great blessing in any boat when water is low or she has to be left as on this occasion away from the usual mooring.

Oars and rowlocks concealed in the bracken, we turned our backs to the wind, glad enough to have something solid under foot and content to carry between us about twenty-five pounds in ten sea trout and a salmon got most unexpectedly on a very 'bad' day. You never know do you?

The River Mouth –
Another Hebridean Day

Take the boat to the far end of the home loch, cross a very soggy moor and climb a high rock-strewn ridge where shoulders of exposed gneiss show deep striae from the passage of Atlantic ice in ancient time and the main hill is before you. Lush grass, deep blue-green in July, and sere and yellow almost overnight in September fills the small glen and then you have a thousand feet of scramble to the shoulder of the hill and your objective is in sight – four miles away. Four miles of walking as good as you can find in this landscape of bog and scree and boulder-filled gullies. In June the golden plover pipe sadly about you and on the heather there are the grouse, quieter now than later on, and the eagles and if the flies are not bad, the deer.

It is a grand walk with the mountain wind in your face and a very hot one when it is at your back. Half-way is a big rock atop a pile of lesser rocks and here in a cool mossy cavity reposes a small stock of canned beer. Here you sprawl in the heather, bags and cased rods laid aside for five minutes, and the ghillie produces an opener . . . For this is the recognized route to the somewhat distant loch which embodies a fishing ground known as 'the river mouth'. There are many river-mouths, one or more on most lochs in that landscape of lochs, and some of them carry a good stock of salmon in due season. But when you say 'the river mouth' hereabouts you mean just this one – the one that awaits you at the end of your walk. So you bury the cans (how I wish everyone would do so everywhere), pick up your gear and the stride that gets you best over rough ground, and go on. Forty minutes on and the loch is at your feet with the boat on the beach far below and your fishing ground shining beyond the low headland of chocolate peat where the river comes out of the hills through grassy flats. A momentary pause to take in the sweep of loch and hill and glinting waves and little crescents of golden beach and you are going down, faster now, to the boat.

One September day it fell out just as I have written it, as indeed, it has happened to me, I am glad to say, many times. I had for company an old friend, Donald, one of the best ghillies, big, thoughtful and serious and handy with a boat. It was noon and the breeze was strong but not too strong and blowing straight on to the river mouth. Now this river is the main spawning feeder for the loch – though there is a bigger river entering elsewhere – and here as the season progresses there is a mounting accumulation of fish. They lie in anything from ten feet of water to a foot or so, not only directly off the point of entry of running water but perhaps a hundred yards either side of it. With a strong wind along the shore they will move one way or the other but always downwind. A *light* breeze along the shore, or an onshore wind of any strength has no effect and the salmon will be in their usual place.

The bottom is hard, graded from fine sand inshore, through coarser stuff to small pebbles thirty yards from the beach. Clean and golden brown it is a good bottom for fish. Salmon do not like foul ground though they will lie very close to reed beds and even in among sparsely grown ones. They do not like soft peat or a weed-covered bottom. It is conceivable that there may be some oxygen deficiency in such places; there certainly is when a foul silty bottom stirs up with a big rolling wave. Such a condition will put fish 'off' just as some peat water will, but this 'sickness' only lasts till the humus-laden water settles again. And it is worth remembering, by the way, that a drop in air temperature, e.g. a cold night, will settle dirty water quicker than anything. The cold may not be in direct effect good for fishing, but will clear the water. I could tell you the tale of a day when a nineteen-pound fish in the boat drove home to me the usefulness of a cold air on silt-laden water but I must not.

I am back, instead, forty yards offshore perched on the board across the stern while Donald sidles the boat crab-wise and island fashion towards the beach. Fish were showing very quietly – head-and-tailing – a back showing here and there in the wave troughs. A nice lot of fish here this September day and we hoped plenty of cocks among them – the big rusty fish that fight harder than spring fish and fight, what is more, right up to the boat and the moment of netting. We found one almost at once; I put the fly within three feet of him and he turned like a flash and had it, the tail and a small Hairy Mary. We led him away from the good water and because I thought the bulk of the fish might go off the head-and-tailing mood I gave him some 'stick' and soon had him coming to the net head up and sliding helplessly.

Donald shipped his oars, put the big net out and the bag floated! The dropper caught in the dry meshes, pressure on the fish eased at once, he turned aside and with a little jerk was gone. It was a stupid thing that should never happen to two old hands. A net of untreated cord such as this one should never be carried dry; however dim the prospects, every net should be wetted as regular routine before the first cast of the day. Donald knew it and so did I and we turned back to our fishing with very little said but both a little thoughtful. Five minutes and three rises later I had another fish and this one we boated without incident, a nine-pound cock, beaked and a bit rusty but a 'smoker' such as we like at the end of the season. I began to think we might have a big day because as yet we had not touched the best of the water, that right in the path of the outflow from the river. Fish there certainly were and every sidle shorewards produced a rise or two. The breeze stayed with us and a good short brisk wave. I could have wished for more breaks overhead but I have seen fish taking well on worse days. Changes of fly, up to fours and down to tens, made no difference; fish rose with soft ineffective boils and not a single one took hold. Fast or slow, dropper sunk or tripping – it made no difference. We did not go too near but after a second time over the water the fish went down and in late afternoon we retired completely defeated. The tally was nineteen fish risen, two hooked and one killed. I did not then know why these fish rose without taking and I don't know now. I am only certain that they could not have been treated more gently – the tackle was very light indeed and the fly thrown from afar and carefully. And it was not fly size that was wrong.

The moral to me can only be that however extensive one's experience of the water, whatever the degree of one's skill in choice and presentation and however good conditions are, there are times, in places full of fish, when one simply cannot catch them. No angler has an unbroken record of successes, and failures usually though not always carry a lesson. Sometimes, as in this case, it demonstrates only how much there is to know.

Attitudes and Conservation

It has always seemed natural and understandable to me that the known and characteristic instability of animal and bird populations must be equally applicable to fish in general and to salmon and sea trout in particular.

True, our judgment of migratory fish populations can only be based on the evidence available to us which is, in general terms, the size of the runs. We can have no basis for estimation of deep sea stocks. All we can know of salmon and sea trout salt water populations is derived from observation of estuary or river mouth stocks, which will be feeding stocks of sea trout, mainly finnock and small adults, and of salmon due to run and collecting in wait for running water.

In some years a run will fail to appear and anglers throughout that river system will speculate as to why. Sometimes, very occasionally, it is possible to pinpoint an answer – a bad spawning season – shortage of spawners – an untimely flood plus frost or the like the appropriate number of seasons previously – or perhaps sheer lack of water. In the latter case, the fish may have fallen victim to estuary nets – or they may run late – too late for angling or observation.

In the case of sea trout, spawning usually every year after maturity – the reason for a run failure is infinitely harder to identify because a sea trout run will, if we exclude the early-running large fish, consist of mixed classes – finnock and small and medium class adults. These fish are, of course, the product of a number of spawning seasons and almost all, including a small percentage of finnock, will themselves spawn. It is admittedly true that generally the peak of the finnock run tends to occur after the peak of the adult run, but once the summer run of spawners gets under way there will always be a large number of immature fish mixed in it.

Poor sea trout runs are known of course, and there are few river systems where fluctuation in numbers is not evident in the records of the years. If we accept that instability of population in wild life is related for the most part to instability of food supply and hence of its character then we can argue with some reason if not with complete conviction, that a 'failure' of food supply in the usual haunts of feeding and growing sea trout will delay maturity in maiden fish and 'ripening' in older sea trout. A direct result could be failure to turn up at the appropriate season at the river mouths. Whether sea trout failing to find normal feeding conditions inside their normal range of feeding movement go far afield in search of more plentiful feed, I do not know, but I am pretty confident that they do and that this often underlies their late – perhaps after the fishing season – arrival in their rivers. It is a proven fact that big sea trout do travel far and I think this is why they are so often mixed with spring salmon.

What then of the short-absence fish – the finnock, herling, whitling, sprods or school peal? These fish have been in salt water for a few months only and in that time have assuredly not been far from the river of their birth. Indeed we know from study of their habits that the smaller sea trout whether immature or mature, are mainly estuary feeders, though some may wander quite far along adjacent open sea coasts. One can hardly argue that such fish will find themselves far from the river at their due running time. Even with a food shortage to drive them away I feel that the proximity of the river is too strong an attraction for them. Thus, with these considerations weighed, we are driven to the conclusion that whilst rich feeding may draw the larger, older classes of fish to more distant waters and result in non-runs or very late ones – we must look elsewhere for the reason behind the non-appearance at due time of finnock and young classes of sea trout.

Some observations in the season of 1968 have led me to the belief that a quite different factor may account for the absence of small fish – the 'condition' of the water supply in the river and its effect on the estuary where the fish feed in spring and early summer and collect prior to running in July and August. Water 'condition' in this context means its temperature and oxygenation.

We are all familiar with low water conditions in the ordinary sense and agreed on the desirability of a spate to aid the running fish but after some sea trout study (I caught my first sea trout in the summer of 1910) I know that determined sea trout will run in very low water and at night will struggle through the thinnest of stickles to populate a river unless stopped by some absolutely impassable barrier. Fish up to, say, two pounds will wriggle upstream in incredibly thin water and I have many times watched them doing so. In 1968 I watched and waited for them to do so in two rivers in the Outer Hebrides – and they did not!

A few came in and the catch in the peak months of July, August and September was one half of average but the big runs normal for these two rivers never materialized. The season was extraordinarily dry for the normally wet islands and at one stage salmon were dying in numbers in the small bare rocky pools of one river where they lay in blazing sun and stale, very warm water. Most of these fish, brought in by a small quickly spent fresh, already exhibited the white spot which develops in bright sun and high temperature in shallow sandy estuaries if the fish are held up by lack of water in which to run. A few sea trout were there, but of course would find shade more easily than the bulkier salmon and apparently suffered less.

But there were not, for all practical purposes, any finnock or small fish in rivers where normally the pools are paved with them and where eagerly-taking finnock are a nuisance. One sea-pool, where normally hundreds of ten- to twelve-ounce fish come in with every tide, carried a few scattered individuals and the run had not arrived when I left the scene in mid-September. At no time was there so little water that these fish could not wriggle up into the sea-pool at the top of the tide.

Nor is there any evidence that the normal shoals of small sea trout were *absent* from the estuary prior to the establishment of drought conditions though, on the other hand, there is no evidence that they *were* there. The simple fact is that the estuary usually teems with sea trout and their presence is something that the watchers take for granted. The abnormality of the season only became noticeable when the rivers fell lower and lower, the sun blazed day after day and those sea trout which had penetrated the lower portions of the rivers actually went back to sea!

I know something about 'false' runs of sea trout which occur at various seasons and from which many return to sea after quite considerable penetration into the river systems. But the fish which comprise the main run in all rivers are true runners which do not return to salt water en masse when behaving normally.

In 1968 in the Hebridean river I speak of, this happened. Those fish struggled into the river and found the low, stale, warm water so repugnant to them or so inadequate for their needs as to cancel out their driving urge to press on. They turned tail and went back to sea. Thereafter the finnock, numerically the strongest class, were there in small numbers, the small adults from one to one-and-a-half pounds were totally absent and the average weight of the several hundred fish caught on the fly went up to about two pounds though, as already noted, the total catch in numbers fell to half the average.

The area concerned is one of heavy rainfall and sustained hot sunshine and consequent droughts are very rare. Local races of both salmon and trout do not meet, and I suggest are not adapted to meet the conditions of the summer of 1968. Fish native to southern rivers, for example, might be so adapted – their parr years might give them greater tolerance of low, warm water and bright light.

The weather certainly affected such island fish as did run in strange ways. I have already mentioned the white spot on the salmon. These eventually, on the head of the fish in fresh water, become ragged areas of raw, red tissue and I expected to see some secondary infection since in some pools the fish were crowded together, but no fungus was seen on any fish which came to hand.

Both salmon and sea trout did, however, behave untypically from a fishing point of view. Both were incredibly dour and both had suffered, in my opinion, in many ways from long exposure to hot bright sun in the shallow estuaries. They were languid and when they did take the fly – did so at depth. It was rare to see a brisk, fresh rise and this was especially noticeable with the sea trout. A surface fly was almost useless and such fish as came to the net, took the fly only when fished very deeply and slowly. Another feature of a strange season was the willingness of otherwise stiff salmon to take a deep slow fly in dead calm conditions and ignoring it in good fishing wave and light.

The mass return to the sea of sea trout was noted by other observers, men living all their lives by the rivers concerned so that the movement is no fancy of mine. None of us had ever seen it before nor imagined conditions totally intolerable to the fish. As to bad taking, there is a tradition that both salmon and sea trout, held up in the sea and unable to run at their due time or thereabouts, are bad risers and never take. I believe in it.

Apart from reservoir fishing one can see in recent years no increase whatever in fishing facilities, but there has been a vast increase in the number of anglers. It is true that much water has become available since the second world war for rent by hotels, syndicates of anglers and associations following the break-up of large estates on which the fishing was preserved, but again these gains have been more than offset by reduction of fishable water due to pollution, to water abstraction for hydro-electric use and to quick run-off drainage schemes, and for other purposes. Overall and operating in a general sense against the well-being of migratory fish stocks there has been the growth of drift-netting at sea and of Greenland netting. Many salmon carrying British tags have been taken on the Greenland grounds and some considerable toll is being taken of our fish. Incidentally, I do know from personal experience that all the fish taken off Greenland in the early 1950s were not salmon though so classified, but were in fact very large sea-going char. I have handled numbers of these 'salmon' which were marketed as 'grilse'. We are painfully aware that this is not the case today.

However all these considerations may bear on the question and whatever the degree of effect from individual causes, there can be no doubt of the decline of migratory fish stocks and of the prospect of sport with them in the British Isles.

It follows that there must be a duty on every fisherman to play some part, however small, in conserving such stocks as we have, and the ordinary fisherman can indeed do a great deal by following self-imposed rules which are only in line with what I have in other references called the tradition of the sport. A simple example covers the treatment of immature fish. Surely in these days, few, if any are killed deliberately, but careless treatment certainly kills many thousands of parr and smolts and tiny finnock every season.

Indeed, all unwanted fish should be released and I have often done so with heavy and gravid hen salmon in the last weeks of the season. It may be less simple with tough-jawed kelts and for them beaching or the landing-net should be the method, followed by the quickest possible unhooking and return to water in an upright position. Kelts can be a nuisance and an irritation at times but there are few sights, in my opinion, more sickening than to see a kelt, however ragged, sinking, done, helpless and bleeding. Sometimes it cannot be avoided but a nagging memory of it can stay with one all day. It is not by any means certain that it is necessary to save kelts since the percentage returning from subsequent sea stay is so small, but that six or seven per cent is worth saving; a few will return.

On this theme of conservation, which in this special context really means fishing improvement, I want to put in a strong plea for reduction in the killing of finnock or whitling or sprods or whatever the small first return from sea and usually immature sea trout are called. Size has to be the only practicable waterside guide, but it is possible that a fat pounder may still be a finnock and no doubt, in my time, I have quite happily put many such fish in the bag. I do not think one can object to this, but I do think there is every objection to the killing of finnock between half and three-quarters of a pound and on some rivers, especially in Scotland, immense numbers of seven- or eight-ounce fish are taken to the measureless detriment of sea trout stocks. It would not be quite so bad if the fish had had a chance to reproduce their kind at least once, but about eighty per cent of finnock do not spawn. If you leave the finnock, you increase the stock; it's just simply that.

I have heard it argued about finnock as about kelt salmon, that the few saved make little or no difference – cormorants, seals, saithe, otters and hundreds of predators are waiting in river, estuary and sea, and man is the least predator. I do not agree. The seals, otters and the predatory estuary and sea fish have always been there and they and their prey have usually been in balance. It is man that has upset the balance.

Learning about fish and how to catch them is a long business in which the beginning of proficiency is fostered partly by inclination and partly by environment and opportunity. It seems to me that in early years one is devoted to fishing without really understanding why and experience merges unobtrusively into a background, as yet confused, of growing knowledge. This was certainly true in my case and I know now that my days and nights by and on the water and what I did to get my fish, were never consciously analysed. I took what came along and, deeply interested, absorbed all of it without awareness that I was putting down, as it were, basic stock in a storehouse of waterside perceptions that was to yield up its useful items on demand over later years.

Very much later came the realization that unwittingly and by great good fortune I had acquired an inexhaustible source of happiness that was mine for the rest of my days. And the factor in my fishing life which has contributed most to this state has been, as all fishermen come to know, the ingrained habit of watching and noting all the natural elements big and small that make up the world of a man who is fishing.

Everyone who goes fishing does so presumably, because he likes it and therefore must to some extent be contented in doing it but I wonder how many today are happy in the entirety of it. So many, it seems, go out to catch fish without discrimination in method, without basic knowledge of the fish and without eyes for the entire world of nature in which, unless they bend their minds to assimilate and be assimilated, they are no more than intruders. When they cease to be that and become instead deeply conscious of all the loch or the river have to offer, they have gained something beyond price, because it is theirs for life.

A good angler is almost always a good amateur natural-ist. He need not know Latin names for wild creatures, flowers or insects, but he needs to know about otters and elvers and why insect-feeding birds feed here and not there, why some types of vegetation grow in some waters and on some shores and not in other places. He must be able to smell weather, to have an eye for wind and cloud and light and most of all perhaps have the ability, understanding currents in loch as in river, to visualize the life of the fish in relation to its environment. He must accept the truth that the last of the ice ages plus subsequent erosion of the landscape, gave us the natural fishing, both locality and quality, that we have today, so he has to be a little of a geologist too. None of these things are difficult to anyone of an inquiring and open mind and the absorbing thing about such studies is that far from interfering with the pursuit of fishing, they are part of it. If a man cannot pause long enough to watch a kingfisher flash upstream, to listen to the crooning of the pigeons in the firs on the far bank, to ponder why the current swings away so sharply in mid-pool or to turn over the pebbles in the shallow and study the larval life revealed, he will not make a fisherman. He will just be a man with rod and tackle and some plastic bags to carry home the fish.

The old writers used to talk about the brotherhood of angling and fellowship of the craft and one smiles at the naïveté of it in these harsh times, but I know and I am sure every lifetime angler knows, precisely what they meant and that they were speaking, in their time, of a reality. The reality has been banished, I greatly fear, by some men because, to begin with, they have not taken in the background of fishing, and are largely unaware of the things I have been trying to outline – they haven't got the craft in their blood. Even more to be regretted, they have not absorbed the traditions, customs, and above all the manners to which the 'brotherhood' subscribe and which made angling in truth the gentle art.

This has nothing to do with social status. I have met by the waterside labourers who were the salt of the earth, and tycoons whose fishing habits and manners revolted me and made me long to be somewhere else. I have been the unwilling guest of a man who owned superlative and exceedingly productive sea trout fly water and who caught all his many big sea trout with float tackle and maggots. His keeper said quietly one day, 'We don't get many fly men here – it's a treat to see it.' His employer did not know until I pointed it out that he had three grilse among the sea trout in his catch. He had been fishing for ten years without any real interest in the fish. By my measurement he gets from his fishing the merest fraction of the pleasure that his opportunities could yield. But whether a man is wealthy enough to own a famous fishing or whether he frequents hotel or club or municipally-owned water makes little difference – this strange tradition-less and manner-less new school deprives itself of the best joys in fishing and spoils it for the rest of us.

One should not be hidebound by convention in fishing techniques, convinced that a new generation is deficient in one's own imagined qualities nor, for that matter, certain that one's own standards are right; and I like to imagine fishermen of my age try to keep impatience in check and try to be fair, trying out and using new methods when they seem to be good. But good manners and sound standards do not change. This said, I can add that it cannot be too much to plead that the manners and customs of a sport such as fishing, proved to be in its interest and of those who follow it, should be maintained and some effort made to adhere to and preserve them. But I see little sign of it. Too many new anglers today wade crashingly into fishing like they blunder into a pool, destroying their chances and those of any unfortunate enough to feel the effects.

I have drifted from a plea for study of how to get the maximum joy out of fishing by being part of the background of the sport and understanding something of all that goes to make up that background, into an apparent fulmination against lack of manners. It is this latter, I think, a symptom of current attitudes on many waters, which hurts the 'brotherhood' – I have to use this word – more than anything. It destroys my pleasure and that of most of my kind when, for example, a boat quite deliberately crosses a few yards downwind of me while drifting on the loch. Such things are commonplace today but they are downright boorish and rude and as great an injury to the craft of fishing as throwing picnic rubbish in the river or littering the banks with it and leaving yards of discarded nylon about or in behaving in any of the other amenity-destructive ways so disgusting to the next man along.

I am afraid of the minority who do these things because it seems that the standard, once depressed, does not rise again and the habit spreads, because such resistance as there is comes from a disappearing generation who will know what I have been trying to say – that fishing is a great deal more than going out with some tackle – preferably ultra modern and very glittering; and a determination to catch something. Sea trout and trout and salmon and the finer ways of catching them are the love of my live, but I have caught a great many pike and there are few things in angling better, in my view, than early morning tench fishing. Whether, however, the troubles that beset game fishing are found in coarse fishing today, I do not know. The litter bugs and the very thoughtless ones are assuredly there.

I seem to have developed a theme the main burden of which is to say what, in my view, is wrong with angling today. But this was not done by intent; my plea is, rather, for more respect for the traditional view of the sport and the medium in which it is carried on – to the great benefit in terms of enjoyment of those who fish for pleasure. Intolerance is a poor thing in a fisherman and an open trap for the older generation. But criticism of fishing standards and practice and manners is not confined to my generation and I have multitudes of friends of all ages who share in my views.

There is greater strain on our angling resources today than ever before and there are many thousands of new would-be fishermen every season. It is vitally important for the well-being of the sport that aspiring brethren should be shown that the fellowship of angling is not open to the pot-hunter and the thoughtless.

Irish Interlude

One of the infinite joys of fishing resides, for my taste, in the extraordinary range of characters one meets, more or less picturesque in word, deed or appearance. Millionaires whose fishing garb can be valued in shillings and poor men 'correctly' attired, men with dilapidated gear who catch fish and beautifully equipped others who do not. However it shows itself, the personality of the man usually emerges in the boat, by the riverside, where everyone eats, drinks and sleeps, or wherever the atmosphere is all fish and fishing. There is a special enjoyment in real whole-hearted fishing which comes from mixing with other anglers, ghillies and countryside characters whose ways are all on or about the waters. Every so often one meets a real 'character' though I confess I seem to see fewer of them than was once the case; perhaps I am not as perceptive.

Years ago in Ireland, at the spring fishing particularly, 'characters' abounded and in those few weeks life on or about river and lough could be a riot of eccentricities and a sheer delight if you had an eye for personality and a suitable sense of humour. The utter inconsequence of minor happenings in the more remote parts of the country and the beautifully quiet and slow tempo of life generally, set the scene of course.

Our circle was small and made up of certain village worthies and of visitors of such long standing and so well known as to be accepted almost as local inhabitants. There was much keen if under-cover rivalry among we fishers on the lough and the small village hotel was ever in a buzz of salmon talk, some of it coming rather ponderously from two elderly legal gentlemen of serious mien and of great repute in Dublin. Inseparable, they fished together daily, the large Mr Campbell in a stern well down with poundage and authority, and the small Mr Gorman in the airy bow. They employed a ghillie from some miles away and as a result we heard little of the goings-on in that boat but they did bring in occasional fish.

Mr Campbell, as befitting his age, rank and seniority among us, presided each evening at the head of the dinner table, having previously applied himself to the contents of a special bottle of the crayther which he and his partner favoured and of which our inn proprietor once said, 'Shure you wouldn't be usin' ut to take the paint off a cart.' Mr Campbell had an enduring complaint about a mouse which haunted him and the fact that he was forced to sleep clutching a walking stick. This special mouse, among the hundreds that infested the place, was wont to comb his whiskers and perform his general toilet in the small hours seated comfortably on Mr Campbell's chest – undeterred by the heavings, or the whisky-laden snorts or by nightly swipes of the walking stick. This by the way. Some of the conversation that adorned those dinner sessions ought to be preserved, but this is a book about fishing and I must confine myself to one example and incident.

It occurred one night when the house dog – an unkempt cocker spaniel – seldom seen 'above stairs' invaded the dining-room and seated himself abreast of Mr Campbell's chair, gazing fixedly at that gentleman and refusing to 'get along wid yez'. I wondered momentarily whether under the pompous bulk there lay the kind heart of an animal lover and the dog knew it. Not a bit of it – furious ringing of the bell presently brought an agitated maid. 'Nora,' growled our chairman, 'take that dam' dog away. I think he's out of his mind. He just sits and stares at me and I'm beginning to wonder if I have a right to me own dinner!' 'Ah well sorr,' said Nora, ''tis aisy to ondherstand in a way. Ye see we had a big upset below in the kitchen wid the crockery all broke an' Nipper here knows ye have 'is plate!'

Out on the lake we often had Father Dermot the village priest, a remarkable character of ever-changing enthusiasms – at that time concentrated on fishing. He had sold his collection of photographic gear and accumulated a house full of clocks which he had sold to buy an ancient and very bruised car presently traded for a boat (oddly enough a good boat) and fishing gear. Every free hour found him fishing alone and I only ever saw him hook one fish. I was lunching in the lee of a hillside wall with my ghillie John one day and Father Dermot was fishing in the bay below us, sitting as usual in the stern so that the wind caught the cocked-up bow and swung the boat all ways. It was so foolish that our amusement turned to irritation and I ceased to watch until roused by John saying, 'Begob, Father Dermot's in a fish!' He was. The breeze was light and the fish very helpfully stayed reasonably near the boat, which with the fisherman so far aft simply rotated on its stern and turned with the fish. Father Dermot held on and as the fish circled so he rotated on *his* axis – long black coat-tails in the water at the stern. Somehow in the turmoil his broadbrimmed black hat went overboard and bobbed away downwind. Then everything went fairly quiet. We could see the bent rod but no sign of a splashing fish though there was at one stage some scrambling forward in evident search for the gaff. There was a certain amount of standing up and sitting down again and of coat-tail dipping and after half-an-hour we concluded we had better see whether we could help. Father Dermot, after a few weeks' fishing, knew it all and was apt to treat advice as a reflection on his skill and vast experience. We pushed off and I took the oars while John prepared to transfer to the priest's boat. 'Can John gaff him for you, Father?' I asked. 'He can,' came the answer, 'if I can get the divvle up.' The fish was somewhere under the rod-tip and that was almost in the water: we backed up on the opposite side and John climbed in while I pulled quickly away. 'Ye'd better get him from under the boat, Father,' I heard John say and the complete angler's reply, 'Easier said than done, me boy, but he'll come to no harm. Sure, he's been under there this last ten minutes.'

The end of that episode was the gaffing of a very tired twenty-pounder. And the last time I saw Father Dermot he walked into a friend's house where, in the larder, the friend and I were packing a salmon in rushes – incidentally the finest packing of all to keep a fish in condition if the rushes are thick, green and long enough. 'How is your anti-poteen campaign going?' I asked the priest who had, I knew, been conducting a drive against the illicit distilling of spirit by the wild boys of the neighbourhood. 'Fine,' said he, 'ye won't find a drop in the parish.' A two-gallon jar of the stuff sat on a shelf within a foot of his nose while he spoke and the situation appealed to me greatly: my friend said later that for his part it had him 'destroyed entirely'. Apart from anything else, the police-station was next door.

Fishing was the main topic of conversation in *that*

establishment too for the sergeant in charge, a quiet man from Connemara, was a keen and highly proficient trout fisher. Between us we took some bags of trout of high average weight from the small river behind his office – he by orthodox wet fly and I on the drifting nymph fished downstream on a loose line. Before I knew our sergeant well, his early-morning perambulations used to puzzle me. Sometimes he quite clearly put in an hour on the river, but usually he passed my window on the stroke of seven-thirty, heading smartly up the village street. In five minutes he would be back at half the pace and always with hands clasped and wrists crossed behind him. One morning I put my head out after he had just passed and beheld in each clasped hand – an egg. He became famous after an incident one Easter-time. There had been the spring races and the village in the evening was full of wild men with money to spend or losses to drown and the three 'hotels' had ranged barrels of porter round their yards – the bars would not hold a fraction of the crowd – and there was drinking and pleasant fighting and lots of fun. With a friend I was paying a social call on the sergeant when a panting small boy arrived to say 'they were after killin' one another in Dooley's yard'. The quiet Connemara one broke off the tale he was telling of a salmon in the main river, put on his uniform cap and departed. He was back in a very few minutes, put his cap carefully on its shelf and with a little hand-dusting gesture said, 'Now phwere was Oi at?'

In those few minutes he had quelled a rather serious fight without his two guards – busy elsewhere – by wading in and speedily cracking the contestants' heads together to knock the fight out of them.

Fifty miles away from that village and its adjoining and very lovely lough is another lough which is not only closely restricted private fishing but has that blessed feature, a run of salmon from April onwards. Not vast numbers of fish but enough to provide a constant chance of a fresh fish. A good run of sea trout comes at June-end – water permitting. I spend as much time as possible on that lough, aided sometimes when my faithful James cannot attend me, by one Thomas. Thomas the strong man, the greatest puller of boats in that county of boat-pullers – Thomas the breaker of oars is a great 'character' with a flair for colourful exaggeration. He once reduced a friend of mine to uncontrollable sniggers by telling him that whilst on good days the salmon would be jostling the boat in their eagerness to get aboard, on a real bad one fishing was as futile as 'T'rowin' peas at the Gineral Post Offis wid the object of demolishin' ut'.

Last spring on a bright windy nor'-west kind of day, I was looking for a salmon on a gravelly shallow near the lough's outlet, with Thomas at the oars. Here the lough floor rises gradually while the shores narrow to the place where the outflowing river begins to exert its pull. Where river ends and lough begins is very thin water flowing swiftly under the arches of an ancient multi-piered bridge and there is, moreover, a long shallow of broken water extending downstream from the bridge. Incoming fish, having struggled through the broken water, quite often settle temporarily just inside the lough before moving into recognized lies up and around the shores. On the day in question I was searching for these fish in a series of short drifts outside the shallow water. I had been having minor trouble with Thomas who wanted me to fish other water about a mile away – the passage thence, of course, giving him opportunity to open his shoulders in the kind of sustained pulling he enjoys. Whether that morning I had more green in my eye than usual, or whether Thomas merely reacted in his own way to my obduracy, I do not know but a simple question from me produced a tale I shall long remember. 'Have you ever seen a really big fish in the lough?' I asked him (our fish average ten pounds and a big one is seventeen or eighteen). Thomas reflected for a moment and then nodded with his chin towards the bridge. 'D'ye see the t'ird arch forninst ye there?' I saw it. 'Well, wan day last winter – December it would be, I was standin' on the bridge and the fish spawnin' on the gravel there – dozens of thim. There was wan in among thim – the biggest salmon iver I saw. T'was a hin fish wid a back as wide as young Kathleen's she-ass. Ye couldn't put a pin between the fish workin' at cuttin' an they was that through other that ye couldn't count thim. The big wan keeps goin' round and round lookin' for a space till she's caught wid her side to the current an she's swep' away an there she is ondher me feet – jammed across the t'ird arch there wid the wather pilin' up and the lough beginnin' to rise. T'was the biggest fish ever I saw.'

Salmon at Dusk

While it is a commonplace in the writings of our sport to say, and truthfully, that fishing takes one into delightful places there are some places which, of their very atmosphere, provide a special lift to the spirit and there is one lough in my dearly-loved Donegal which has this quality above all others. There are other loughs which to me yield more salmon but less joy in being there and in fishing.

No majestic mountains tumble screes to this lough; it lies on low ground chequered by small green fields and gorse-topped banks and along the flat stony shores thickets of bog-myrtle – russet-flowered in the spring. Columba, the turbulent priest-prince who became the gentlest of saints, walked here, and here much earlier Neolithic man built his crannogs and the secret shallow causeways to them where today lurk the best of the lough's trout. Beyond the run of the cultivated ground in the north-west are the tops, softly azure in sun and profoundly blue in shadow, of the high hills. And at one end of the lough, between and around inflowing and outflowing rivers, are acres of reeds, sere and golden at the time of the spring fishing – a green waving jungle in summer. Here are grebes and ducks and otters and sanctuary for any salmon with the wit to make a long, strong run into the fastness. The reeds grow, of course, in the shallows and all along their outer limits fish lie thickly for perhaps two hundred yards out into the lough. But before they do so, entering fish travelling in companies after their eight-mile run from the tide, scatter round the unreeded shores and for a time – hours or days – may be found almost anywhere within half-a-mile of the outflowing river by which they entered. And hereby hangs this particular tale.

It began about ten o'clock on an April morning when with my ghillie John, an old friend, I pushed off from the river mooring and headed out through the reed-walled channel to the lake. Inside the wind-tossed reeds the waves were no more than an even surge; outside on the open lough there was a big lively wave. Wind, unhappily, was due east and the light was uniformly grey and poor though cloud was high. It was cold too, and all things considered it was a singularly unpromising day. It was the more disappointing because the lake was falling quickly after a spate that had, we knew, brought large numbers of fish, the main spring run. They had had two days to settle and with any kind of luck at all with conditions, we were justified in expecting a good day. John pulled fairly close in on the eastern shore and we began a long drift across the reeds into the western bay and the lee shore. Fish plunged here and there and I had one soft ineffective rise as we passed the mouth of the incoming river. Back upwind we had another drift across slightly deeper water. It was admittedly early in the day to expect fish to move in April but the big stock should have provided an odd bolder fish. It did not. I began to look round and further afield. I have a note in my diary which shows that at 12.20 p.m. I looked up and saw an eagle swinging slowly very high over our heads – the only eagle I have seen in all my Irish years.

At one o'clock, we beached the boat on the eastern

shore and lunched out of the wind under the thick gnarled gorse a few feet higher than the lough, the whole fishing area in sight. 'If only' – we said – 'we had a west wind!', but the day looked, if anything, dourer than ever and in fact we fished the afternoon out without seeing the slightest sign of an interested fish. Not surprisingly, the usual afternoon move of trout failed to materialize. In that bitter wind there was no hatch of fly and the overall conditions keeping the trout down were of course affecting the salmon. I always believe that if air conditions will stimulate a rise of trout there is a chance of a salmon. I have seen it happen so very often.

The day so far, however, was not without a certain reward. Three successive drifts ended close in to the shore on the west – with the prevailing wind a lee shore – on which the rollers broke in foam on the stones. Each time we approached the shore we saw plunging fish and they seemed to be concentrated among the submerged ruins of an old shieling – the temporary resting-place, clearly, of a shoal of fresh fish. I fished down to them and among them once without moving a fin and thereafter stayed away lest we should scatter them by putting the boat over such a shallow and limited lie.

At five o'clock I went ashore to sit by the fire and drink hot tea in John's little house. Here soon I was joined by an old friend from the village up the road. Like me, he was haunted by the prospect of a lough full of fresh fish and, despite the weather – now steadily growing worse – and refired by his enthusiasm, I decided to try again. My diary records that we fished, he in the bow and me in the stern, from seven till nine.

We worked across the reeds first, the wave much bigger now and the light going rapidly. Because of both wave and the overcast I went up two sizes in the flies, with a

Claret on the dropper and a Thunder and Lightning on the tail, both fours. Down in the corner where the reeds grew thinner as they met the stony west shore I had a good rise, a solid take, and the first fish of the day was on. Hustled a little because we were anxious to get at what John described as 'that nest o' fish' among the old walls, this one, a lovely fresh hen of twelve pounds, came to net fairly quickly.

The light became less and less and very soon we were fishing in a kind of weird dusk lit by dirty yellow gleams from the west where angry blue-black cloud masses parted fleetingly to admit what remained of sunset. Along the shore where we had earlier marked the fish, wind and wave were too heavy to allow us to drift broadside and with the bows half into wind, I in the stern had the best of it. How many fish we rose I do not know. They rose like trout with quick slashes at the fly and the lurching boat made it difficult at times to leave it with them.

My friend had first blood – a ten-pound fish that led us away up-wind before we had him. At the net he did a complicated lash and roll and left the cast hopelessly entangled and possibly weakened. A new one went on while we went back on the drift. Both fishing again we had an immediate demonstration of how clearly a fish can see the fly even in bad light. My friend's tail fly was six inches in the air and about to hit the water when a fish poked his head out of the side of a wave and took it while it was still in the air. We all saw it and the twisting-away snatch that followed. I would not care to say we heard the 'snick' as the fly parted from the cast but the picture was so vivid before us that we imagined we did. Then it was my turn with another up-wind quickly-beaten runner and again of ten pounds. I knew that we should lose one of these active fish sooner or later because strong as John is, it was impossible to move the boat head on in that sea at anything like the fish's speed and one saw backing going and going . . . In that lough too, fish are exceptionally strong and with normal tackle it is quite impracticable to try to stop a fresh fish determined to go. In a light breeze, with easy manœuvrability of the boat, such fish can be turned with sidestrain but not in heavy water. Here we were, wallowing about in near darkness and it seemed that every fish hooked was crazy to get to the middle of the lough.

The next fish my friend hooked was assuredly crazy, running round and round the boat with a peculiar wriggling motion on the surface for all the world like a kelt, though he was a very fresh eleven-pound cock hooked firmly in the tongue. At the first cast, after boating the wriggling one, he had another and this one for a change ran inshore, lashed like a fury in very shallow water and smashed the cast. There was a great deal of dark muttering up in the bow.

It was dark now, as dark, John said, 'as the inside of a cow' and I think we were all becoming slightly insensitive – buffeted by wind and wave and perhaps a little too exhilarated to fish carefully. I know that I missed two or three fish that in daylight I think I would have hooked – the quick splashy rises were difficult to see and worse still to time in the rough water. All the fish came to the Thunder which of course suited the darkness and with his broken cast my companion had lost the last big fly of this pattern he had. I gave him one which later, in the light, turned out to be a Black Dose. He had no more rises but I had a third, rather smaller, fish before I too was broken.

This last fish fulfilled my earlier prediction. I hooked him inside the ruined walls and he shot out past the boat like the proverbial greased lightning. Straight out into deep water he went; the reel screamed and went on screaming while John, nearly beaten now, struggled to force the boat upwind. We went slowly after the fish and for a time the reel was silent and I began to hope. Somewhere about ninety yards ahead in the tossing blackness in the eye of the wind there was a very strong fish. The rod was bent with all the strain the tackle would take and my finger on the line when the rod point was pulled down hard and I *had* to let more line go. Inevitably after that I had to try once more to stop him to save the last of the line and this time the cast gave between dropper and tail and he was gone. I suddenly realized how cold it was.

Half-erect in the lurching boat, we put John in the stern with his feet among the fish, and side by side amidships we fishermen pulled home. I have taken odd fish just before dusk but only odd ones. A take such as I have described, yielding five fish in a bare two hours, much of it in total darkness, is an event.

The Finest Moment in Salmon Fishing

The dropper makes a little broken furrow in the hollow of the waves, is lost in the crest, emerges again, takes colour from the light and looks very right for the kind of day it is. It comes closer to the boat at the bidding of rod and indrawn line and quietly beside it appears a shining brown back and, sail-like, the upper lobe of a tail. The apparition remains etched razor sharp in your mind long after it has slid forward and down leaving the dropper futile in a swirl of water. But the line is coming taut and becomes vibrant as you lift and bend the rod against the hidden thing so strong down there under the wave. That salmon, initially attracted by the dropper, has taken the tail fly and you have hooked him. The ghillie says 'That's a good fish', the day is bright and this to me is one of the great moments in fishing.

The most critical deliberation at the ending of fishing days, and of expeditions, in the review at each season's close, has left me in doubt even after all these years as to what makes up the greatest moment in salmon fishing. The doubt is not mine alone because if you put this question to others you will assuredly get, in about eight out of ten cases, a momentary brightening of the eye, a frown of concentration and finally a hesitant 'I really don't know'. Few are positive – they just 'think' this or that –

they love just simply – and who does not – the process of hooking, playing and landing a fish. It *is* wonderful of course and one enjoys every minute of it, but I for one have always, it seems, been trying to break it down – is it the sight of a rise, the first transmitted sensation of a hooked fish, the first sight of the fish in play, cartwheeling in a storm of broken water, the first sight of a tiring fish pulling quietly in a wave or the current, the sight of the fish in the net or in the boat, on the bank, or what?

You hear of individuals who, having hooked their fish, will hand the rod over to the ghillie and these men have presumably extracted from the event all the pleasure which for them must reside in the raising and hooking. I have never met any of these men but their choice of the supreme moment is at least clear whether one approves it or not.

For my part I put the rise and the hooking in first place only if it takes place slowly enough to be appreciated. Rise forms vary, less with salmon than with sea trout but they do vary. Some, particularly with small very fresh fish, are too fast to be savoured: the water explodes about the fly and the pull comes instantaneously. The shock of surprise does not rob the moment of its drama but to be cold-blooded about it, this type of take (whilst greatly to be sought!) brings no element of anticipation and thus is little influenced by restraint or skill.

But a slow deliberate rise is another thing altogether and something which will test the nerve, which means the experience and skill, of the rod. A slow head-and-tail rise, or the kind of move which displays the fish swimming on the surface in pursuit of the fly – and salmon will do this in some moods – stretches anticipation to the point of agony. It's the slowness that does it. You know that this type of rise usually means a take but not until the fish turns, goes down or away and the line draws tight can you be sure. He may be playing with you or the fly or both of you and this occasionally but not often happens. It does occur, however, when fish are coming 'on' when a short phase of 'following' may precede a general take.

The great beauty of a true and slow head-and-tail rise is the chance it gives you to see the fish as he comes up, arches awash in current or wave and goes down. You see shoulder and curve of back, dorsal and tail one after the other and the lovely tan of the fish – the dark spotted tan that might be that of a very big trout but will, in fact, be blue and mauve and silver and very untroutlike in the boat.

Somewhere under those marching waves a fish takes your tail fly, the solid stop of the fly's progress the only indication. Not so much as a trace of swirl marks the water and the fish, after a moment's wavering movement, goes steadily off. You expect him to increase speed and make a long fast run. But he does not, he just pulls hard and you agree with your ghillie that he could be a biggish fish. You go after him and try to play him at fifteen yards distance: sometimes he comes closer and high enough in the water for you to see the dropper. But he's very strong and keeps boring so that you have to give line and near the finish he's circling the boat – taut line and now and again the upper few feet of the cast cutting the waves. He's coming up though and suddenly you see him, resisting convulsively now, in the side of a wave. There at last is your unseen fighter, flashing bright as he turns and sways – brown and darkly spotted as he surfaces and wallows before weakly trying to run again. He isn't a big fish after all – just a strong well-made fresh fish and the prime of his kind. But what a thing it is to see him there, and clearly for the first time, this vision from the dark water of the lake – this hunter from the wild ocean. You are living one of the greatest moments in fishing for salmon.

There remains, I sometimes think in the midst of my indecisions on the question of the finest moment in salmon fishing, one other event that 'takes some beating' and that will occur in one of those loughs or lochs – for you find them in all the wilder places famous for long running fish. Now there is, of course, no real rule anywhere about this. One fish will make prolonged runs in course of play, another will not, yet the fish in some places are prone to it and none more likely than fresh but rested ones. Your stale fish is more likely to be hard fighting in a dour way. It is significant that water which tends to produce long running fish is shallow and level bottomed so that fish cannot go deep and there plug away head down.

These runners can have you in an agony of anxiety because you have no control whatsoever with fifty or sixty yards of drowned line and backing out. Line goes and goes and you keep a firm but not harsh hold while the boat gathers way in pursuit. It does not matter that the behaviour of the fish has given fair warning – that from relatively quiet play, perhaps too near the boat, he starts to go away. Up to a point that move is all to the good but suddenly he accelerates and he keeps going. But then more and more line appears – he's coming up. Now is the moment, for he does one of two things – he either lashes about in the waves and goes down again and you see very little of him – or he jumps magnificently and you see all of him in one flashing picture in which you try to lower the rod. He's so far away that you wonder if he can be *your* fish but recovering line now you feel him again. You boat this fish and that is a good feeling. But the supreme 'moment' was the five seconds when he was 'up' and you could see him – the fish you had conjured from the lake by exercise of 'the art of tempting the unknown with a fishing line'.

So, at the end of a good day – water-proofs and heavy boots shed, face burning with a day's wind or sun or rain or all of them, and perhaps glass in hand, you live it again. You look up and see the black-headed gulls and the terns heading north in the evening light towards nestlings waiting on the isles – each adult with a beakful of sandeels. The direct purposeful flight of precisely regular wing beats has a curious grace.

You look down to the grass, softly touched now by coming dusk and to your shining salmon. This, too, is a moment very surely dear to your heart.

Lough of the Crannog

If you fish in Ireland, or in parts of the Highlands and Islands, you will add to your pleasure if you can take some little interest in archaeology. Naturalist or student of nature you *must* be wherever you fish and you cannot be a fisherman in the full sense of the word unless you are. But some small understanding of archaeology is *not* necessary – it merely adds interest to your doings in country where there are prehistoric hut circles, lake-dwellings and other traces of ancient peoples whose pre-occupation like yours was the taking of fish. The direct link with your fishing is, of course, tenuous but it is both truthful and not stretching the point too far to say that over the years some hundreds of trout and sea trout must have gone into my bag because of recognition of lake-dwelling sites and their underwater features.

Actually it bears the name of an Irish saint, this lough of my story and I had no idea until I saw it that it contains the best example of an Iron Age artificial island, a crannog, of the many I know. The country in which it lies is dotted with loughs large and small, bog-fringed and peaty for the most part. Some are unapproachable, the margins floating mats of vegetation which slowly sink underfoot; one makes half-a-dozen casts to rising trout and must then flee to firmer ground. Some pools on the high ground are hard-bottomed and weedless and here and in the peat loughs the trout are small and dark: any team of small flies will catch them three at a time. Big trout are those of a pound or over but in a few places there are really big trout; I know of a worm-fishing small boy who produced from a piece of sacking in the village one evening, three lovely trout each over four pounds.

I heard about the lough named after the saint, during a talk about big trout. It was the property of the owner of a pub in a nearby village, and so private that even gentlemen in dog-collars were not permitted to fish. The owner, I was informed, was 'a cross man – as cross as a bagful of weasels'. He had stocked the lough, an unheard of thing in those parts, years before and there it was: he did not fish and he did not allow anyone else to fish. Legend had it, of course, that there were enormous trout there. I proposed to make friends with the cross one and was strenuously discouraged in any such venture: I would return, I was assured, with a very large flea in my ear. But I called at the hotel, where the purchase over the bar of enough wine of the country to float a curragh, and the undertaking to do the landlord some trifling service in England, gained me the freedom of the lough for one day. I did not find him a cross man at all; in fact towards the end of the evening he actually produced 'me private bottle' containing amber liquid fifteen years old and we became distinctly friendly. I was bidden to take the boat – 'She's a grand boat, the best ever to come out of Rathmullen.'

My ghillie John knew where the lough lay in a jumble of small rough hills out on the moor but I was totally unprepared for what I saw when we reached it through thickets of scrub hazel curtained with hanging lichen and acres of tumbled boulders hidden in old rank heather and bracken. Steep-sided, the lough occupied a small hanging valley and covered perhaps ten acres. An ancient glacial outflow was marked by a low mounded ridge across the only gap in the skyline when I looked across the lough from the water's edge and I could see the moor far beyond and below. We had intersected the shore almost at the north end and here it was low and reedy. A deeply-indented bay lay to the right and another, apparently filled with lily-pads, ran in towards the overflow gap. One could fish the shore at the outflow but nowhere else. Nine-tenths of the shoreline was under boulder-filled undergrowth and very steep, or was forty-foot cliff as smooth and vertical as the wall of a house. Immediately before me, forty yards from shore and across the mouth of another bay was a small oval island, tree-clad and scrub-shrouded, which looked like a typical crannog.

It was a nice evening in May, clear and warm but the breeze was all over the place bringing a ruffle from one quarter and then another. It did not look promising though I had been warned that it was useless to fish before dark when the absence of breeze would matter least; the thought of the salmon I had had that morning from the big lough was sustaining. Odd trout were showing far out presumably taking sedges blown out from the shore. The water was extraordinarily clear with a greenish tinge unusual in that part of the country.

We found in the reeds 'the best ever to come out of Rathmullen'. She was resting on the bottom with only the gunwales above water and without sign of oars or baler. Search of the undergrowth produced two odd oars minus leathers and a rusty paint can which would serve to bale and eventually a very rotten boat was floating. We con-ceded that at some time she had been a good boat. Now she leaked like a basket and if one allowed her to fill again she would sink like a stone. The worst leaks were plugged with pieces of rotten mooring rope and keeping booted feet on main frame members we pushed off in the certain knowledge that a foot on unsupported planking would go straight through.

Without knowledge of the water, I put up a test cast with small Mallard and Claret on the tail, Corncrake Sedge on the dropper and Butcher on the bob, and by the island we started to fish. There was insufficient breeze for a drift and I threw a long line from a quietly moved boat. Occasional fish showed but none within reach and I fished blind towards the overhanging branches and trails of honeysuckle on the island where I presently had a deep quiet rise. I played the fish while John baled out some of the rising water and he had done so and taken to the oars again before the fish was ready for the net. I have never seen a better trout for shape, condition and colour. It was a short deep fish – sparsely spotted red and black, of clear golden yellow on sides and belly and an obvious three-pounder. This was good.

Before moving elsewhere I had a closer look at the island and there, plain to be seen going down ten feet into the clear water were the great timber piles, oak probably, that held the island together. The Iron Age people who made these crannogs nearly 3,000 years ago, often used walls of piles to contain the brushwood, rocks and earth piled inside them but usually the piles have sunk or rotted or splayed out and now lie flat and the island sinks lower as the ages pass. This was a good example of the uncause-wayed lake-dwelling: I could find no trace of the under-water track of stones connecting crannog with shore that form a feature in some loughs and provide, where they are long enough (some may be 100 yards) good shallow fishing ground. Some of these causeways have twists and breaks in them, clearly to mislead an enemy who might identify the shoreward end and seek to cross. Sea trout and trout find these artificial reefs much to their liking and I always fish over and around them when wind and wave will permit. I know one at least where salmon lie, the irregular stony track, now carrying two feet or more of water, always holding a few fish. The archaeological diversion thus I hope justified, I must return to the events of the fishing I am describing.

The area round the island did not produce any more rises and I baled furiously while John pulled across to the bay of the lily-pads. The light was going and with sunset we lost the wind: the cliffs and high ground above them cut off the light from most of the lough and left it a still pit of gathering blue shadows. It had had a curious sombre air in full light and now out on it in a sinking boat in the nearing dark I decided, childishly, that I did not really like it, in spite of the beauty of that trout drifting round in the water at my feet.

But I went on working the flies slowly and deeply in the calm and expecting some sort of general night rise to begin at any time. On the edge of the lily-bed, I had another take – a fish of about two pounds this time but light-coloured and bright like the first. After that there was no sign of life and the lough was utterly still. We put the boat's nose on the beach behind the reed bed, baled again and considered. 'If there *are* big trout here,' I said to John, 'they should move in the next half-hour and we should give them a try. You watch the water level and I'll fish a really big deep fly.' It seemed reasonable enough and I mounted a cast with a single big fly – a number six Dusty Miller. In retrospect it seems a strange choice of pattern in view of the absence of any light at all and I do not now recall my thinking when I selected the fly. I do know, however, that it was one of the queer variety of

Dusty that has a lime-green hackle in place of the pinky-flame of the regular dressing.

We moved out towards the centre of the lough and into, presumably, deep water. There on the edge of the hill's inky shadow I began to work the big fly with slow line-fingering. The boat would go quietly with a touch of the oars for so long and then become loggy as she filled and we would have to bale and move on to an undisturbed area. We could never bale her out and we counted her dry with five or six inches of water round our feet – baling at any lower level the paint can banged on the ribs and in that still pool we needed utter quiet. In that quiet we could hear that most elusive sound of early summer night in that country, the croak of the flighting woodcock among the taller trees, and the gabble of duck off the nest to feed and splash along the margins.

I was thinking that we had had enough of this place, becoming increasingly eerie and depressing, and of the menace of the sinking boat, when the rod-top slammed down to a solid pull and I was into what was obviously a heavy fish. I got rod and myself into some sort of conventional fishing attitude. I had not with such slow fishing expected any sort of surface take and I had been fishing by feel alone but John, who had not realized how deep the fly was, had been watching and now said he had seen the fish's body and tail as it took the fly. I had not. 'Like a salmon', 'father and mother of all the trout', 'begob he had a tail like a shovel' were expressions I heard in the next few minutes while the fish cruised deep with the reel ticking slowly and John turned the boat with one oar and baled furiously with the other hand. The fish pulled hard and evenly and was about as unyielding as a salmon moving at a speed of his own choosing. The ten-foot rod was hard bent and the line entered the water an oar's length from the boat. We moved away a little but the fish came with us. He kept making little runs but never away from us – always down and deeper. I tried easing the strain to see if less pull on him would induce him to come up so that I could shorten line but this only encouraged him to take more. Nothing I could do with the rod was effective and so much line had gone that we dare not again try pulling away to get side strain, because if he then made a run, we were done. I did not know how much backing there was on the reel. I had thirty yards of running line and some backing and I regularly used it for sea trout fishing when I reckon one is safe with fifty or sixty yards all told. Most of the dressed line was now out.

Any thrill that this battle with a big fish possessed lay in its demonstrations of sheer strength and obstinacy on the part of the fish and however protracted an account of it may be, it will reflect only that. At the end of something like fifteen minutes of circling and holding on – and baling – the line was straight up and down and the fish was right under the rod-tip with thirty yards of line and some backing out. I had a mind's-eye picture of a very big trout indeed cruising in the darkness about a hundred feet under that rotten boat. The thought was all but oppressive; he seemed tireless.

How long he could have circled in sullen strength I shall never know because without variation in the strain and without warning he was gone. Cast and fly were completely in order. We baled the pride of Rathmullen for the last time and paddled her back to her place among the reeds where, as far as I know, she still lies.

I still wonder, sometimes, if I could have handled that fish differently. My handicap was lack of line. One of my salmon reels with a hundred and fifty yards on it would have enabled me, without risk, to make him run . . .

Days from the Diary

The scene is a very small lough in a boggy hollow at the foot of a gorse-covered mountainside in Donegal. This pool, for it is little more, contains trout of exceptional quality, fat and golden and bright-spotted and very hard to reach to raise the fly. Part of the difficulty of extracting these fish from their watery element is that the pool is unapproachable in all but one small space where the shore is stony. Elsewhere is quaking bog – and not risky but downright dangerous. The day in my diary found my ghillie John and me there in bright sun with a wind down the mountain, and off the only hard segment of shore. Now I must tell you that a narrow beach here was backed, quite inconveniently for casting, by a belt of old straggly willows. When we arrived there were no rising fish to be seen but I noticed that when we had a strong puff of wind down the hillside and through the willows, there was a short-lived series of rises out on the pool – something clearly was blown off the trees.

John went a few yards further to beat his way back through the gorse raising clouds of small stuff as he worked back to the willows. We gave it five minutes to settle and I would like to tell you that we made a careful entomological check to see what insect life there was but we did not. I was intent on a silly plan of my own.

John from his position on the far side of the willows took two or three of the supple stems in his hands and carefully pulled them low to the ground, while I with a kind of steeple cast put a dry Greenwell as far out in the pool as I could. Then at a word from me the branches were allowed to spring forward and hurl their insect population across the water. A short but energetic rise developed at once, the little fly was taken and I hooked a fat pounder. We did this successfully four times and then ran out of willows young enough to bend and also out of natural flies.

I remember that on the way back across the bog we found a mallard drake and three ducks neatly cached in thick rushes, presumably by one of the many foxes in that area. We often went bush-whacking after that but it would only work in a dead calm air or with wind down off the hillside and I have never found any other way to catch those lovely trout.

There was a certain dark stony shore on another lough with a reputation for holding big fish. It was dark because the beach stones were mossy and also because a dense plantation of mixed conifers grew close behind the beach. I think the two conditions are related because the trees cut off much of the sunlight from the inshore fringe. Why big fish should prefer this area is one of those salmonoid mysteries beyond solution. It certainly was and is one of the best holding places in the Irish lough and has one recognizable good feature – a dense reed-bed where the hard shore peters out at the south end. In the angle between reeds and shore there are three to eight feet of water and salmon are always here from early spring onwards. It was not much fished because it needs a west wind. A little south in it will not hurt but the west wind is the proper one and we do not get many airs from that quarter at the peak of fishing in early April. There is a little boggy field along this shore where the snipe nest and there is much diving and drumming while you fish and the soothing voices of pigeons in the trees.

I had a fish in the magic half-hour before lunch and afterwards Michael joined me to fish in the bow. John, as always, had the oars, and we were all in good heart because the wind was west and warm and the waves rolled soft and even on the shore. The sun was shining and there was already a fish on the floorboards. There is nothing like a fish in the boat to stimulate good talk and good spirits. We were making short drifts into shore and the water looked so good that I for one expected a rise with every cast. None came and we worked along until we reached the old wall dividing field from plantation. The stones of the wave-wrecked end of the wall reach out into the lough and ten yards off their ending, Michael and I both rose fish and hooked them both.

Now this kind of thing is fine and makes for sport so long as the fish go their separate ways and keep doing just that without going too far. The boat cannot follow both of their runs and the fish simply have to be played by the rods in the manner that seems best minute by minute to keep them (a) from running too hard, and (b) from crossing. If it is agreed to follow one runner the other fish will assuredly resent being pulled unless very slowly and he will run – probably in the opposite direction. In short, whatever one chooses to do is likely to be wrong and the fish share the mastery.

In our case both fish chose to be quiet for a time – light holds contributing to this, and we began to have hope when it became clear that my fish was noticeably smaller than Michael's: it could happen that by application of a

little more 'stick' I could bring mine to the net. I tried it
and the fish did come up – the usual springer of ten pounds
or so. Another moment or two and he would come in but
after going down again he kept on going and worse still,
headed across from left to right. I was helpless to stop
him. I changed the rod's angle to get a little side strain but
he was still too strong to respond and in a flash we had
crossed lines about thirty yards away. The change in pull
seemed to wake up Michael's fish which made a run from
right to left ending in a cartwheel which showed us a big
fish of twenty-five pounds or so. The line was under mine
and now my fish turned back and presumably ran deeper
still because the lines were locked together it seemed,
fifteen or twenty feet from both fish. At this stage I think
I might have boated my fish but the big fellow refused to
come. There was a confused flurry and both lines were
slack – the casts had gone in both cases at the tail fly. We
might have managed it better but I do not know quite
how. It is one of those things simple of solution fishing
by the winter fireside and rather less simple when, sitting
in the boat, two people have to play complementary parts
as well as two wayward salmon. When I see John now he
always says, 'Do you mind the day we hooked the two
fish down the plantation shore?'

There is a lough with a soft Gaelic name between the sea
and the mountains which for me is the lough of the stoats.
It is that scarce thing in moorland – an alkaline water, and
trout are of good quality. I was last there on a dark day
with a wind off the Atlantic that chilled us through,
though it was late April. I had again for ghillie my faithful
John and we had a very few trout for much fishing when
we went ashore to the shelter of a tumbledown wall.
Relaxed out of the wind we took little heed of odd

chirpings among the stones until a stoat put head and shoulders out of a cavity a few feet away, to be followed by another and then more until every chink held a little wicked face. The chirpings grew to a shrill kree-ing. John said, 'The place be's alive with the divules!' and departed. I went too. A solitary stoat comes to my bird table here at home to assist the diary in stirring the memory of that dark day.

A more expansive note records a somewhat involved expedition in the north of Norway.

For a long time I had had an urge to catch char – not the little fellows of our lochs at home but good fish of which I heard tales in Scandinavia and the rest after a conference in Oslo was a very long trip to the north – objective a high lake close to the Swedish border. I know some places at home which are pretty remote but we have nothing as inaccessible as this Norwegian lake. The beginning meant the better part of a night and a day by train and boat to reach our true departure point. Here surplus baggage was left in the village and I found myself with a forty pound rucksack and a bundle of rods and a further day's journey, much of it on foot, before me. There was, it was said, a road part of the way and we boarded an ancient truck driven by a Norwegian with a club foot and no English, up the most appalling track I have ever seen. It climbed, that 'road', for about two thousand feet through thick lichen-draped forest – a narrow shelf of loose stones, potholes and boulders twisting along the mountainside. About every mile we stopped to cool the boiling radiator and refill it from one of the innumerable streams crossing our track.

The trees thinned a little and we presently stopped in a clearing on the edge of a marshy lake where one of the high prowed local boats was waiting. The truck disappeared and we boarded the boat and started off up the lake with a tough-looking young fellow at the oars. The lake was narrow, winding and carried a perceptible current against us, so much so, in fact, that our tough-looking young man was flagging after about an hour. I took the oars and found the boat about half the weight of our Scottish or Irish boats and very easy to pull. We disembarked in a bog, shouldered the rucksacks and ploughed on over very unpleasant going – ancient fallen trees littered the forest floor and my burden felt like sixty pounds. But eventually we emerged on hard ground on the shore of another lake where waited another boat which in half-an-hour landed us at the base of a very steep rocky escarpment and from here on we had to climb. The rucksack became even heavier and I was thankful when we emerged on an undulating plateau of alpine meadows. And here was the saeter – the summer grazing farm which in Scotland we would call a sheiling – which was to be fishing headquarters.

Magnificently fed and cared for in that farm, it nevertheless had for sleeping a small hut on the hilltop a quarter of a mile away and on the fringe of the tree-line. In that dry season of twenty-four hours' daylight I slept with door and windows open wide and mountain air blowing through the hut until one morning I discovered a she bear and partly grown cub just outside. I closed the doors after that. The grassed–over roof carried a magnificent thicket of wild raspberries and I suppose that was the attraction.

The small lakes nearby swarmed with sik which I identified as *Goregonus lavaretus* which we call powan in Loch Lomond and there were some trout, but the fishing I had come so far to seek was six miles farther on and I have vivid recollections of the dense forest which covered most of the route. There was a faint trail and I used to hear the cow bells miles from the farm: what the cows found in dense timber I could never understand. Most disconcerting at first was the crashing clatter of capercaillie leaving the trees overhead.

The lake I had come so far to fish was just above the limit of the trees and occupying a rock basin in the hilltop. The shores were a jumble of broken rocks except in one place where a little meadow came down to the water, growing softer and marshier as one approached the margin. Cloudberries grew in this wet ground, the single berries ripening from bright gold to cherry red in one day's clear sunshine. My daily picking was blended, back at the farm, with sour cream to make a mousse fit for gourmets.

I used to think Lough Salt in Donegal contained clear water, but this Norwegian lake in that respect was almost unbelievable. Depth was impossible to calculate but I reckoned I could see every pebble and tuft of weed in twenty feet of it – perhaps more, and in one place a great fish of ten pounds or over which I took to be a trout. Far out from shore on most days there were occasional rises but never one within reach. The lake and its surrounding terrain were delightful but the fishing was very difficult. I continued to pick up a single fish or a brace of char to small bright flies each day, my best a fish of three pounds. There was, I found, a certain willingness to take each early evening. I threw the longest line possible and now and again a fish would materialize from deep water and take savagely.

There is a peculiar hopelessness in fishing ultra-clear water when from the shore you can see every detail of the bottom far out into the lake because, I think, in the absence of rises the whole scene is so utterly barren. The char when hooked were very strong and active and averaged something like two pounds. So I had caught some on the fly – not as big as I expected but very good char and I had learned a few things.

I made the long trip back to the stifling south contentedly enough though it had all seemed an elaborate exercise to catch a few char.

It was in April on a Donegal lough. I shared the boat with a friend of many years and great frankness of speech. The ghillie was young Patsy, in his early 'teens but bright and keen and handy at the oars. Light and wave were good but the south wind had a chill in it and there were occasional heavy cold showers; we had had three days of this, an odd rise, but no fish. The flies were sixes or sevens to suit the wave and the biggish water – the patterns I cannot recall.

About three o'clock in the afternoon a few trout started to show and I put aside the big rod and took up the little trout rod that I usually had in the boat for just such a contingency. It was eight feet and weighed less than four ounces – built cane by a good maker and a very nice rod. On it was a suitable little reel and light line and I put a Hewitt-stained cast of 5 lbs with three trout flies thereon. They were, I think, twelves and the bob fly was a Mallard and Claret. I had not fished trout since the previous autumn and I took the cast dry from the cast case. Trout were three to the pound in that lough and the dry cast did not seem to present any danger, it would soften and straighten in a few minutes. As it happened, however, the cast was still in coils on the water when at the third cast I had a nice taking rise from a salmon and he was on.

I regard the 'fight' that followed as the most exhausting I have ever had. It went on for an hour and forty minutes while my friend sat huddled and shivering in the bow swearing softly to himself and we proceeded very sedately about half-a-mile up the lough and back again twice. At no time did the fish show or attempt to run. The butt of the toy rod was vertical and the tip most of the time in the water. The fish swam steadily six feet from the boat and I had acute cramp in my rod hand because the cork grasp was so very slender. Twice that fish passed within feet of a big sunken thorn bush but went steadily on. I became very tired of him and wanted to stir him up and create some action or lose him – I did not care which, but my crew protested and Patsy said we would get him for sure. At last I could take no more of it and told Patsy to stand by with the gaff. I applied a fraction more pressure, expecting something to go very suddenly, and up rolled the fish. Patsy made no mistake and in seconds we had a fresh sixteen-pound cock in the boat.

My friend duly recovered but the rod never did; it was strained far beyond recovery. Two things more about the tackle. The reel had, we later found, fifteen yards of line on it and the cast was stretched in one place to the thickness, quite literally, of gossamer thread. How it held that fish I cannot imagine. Was this affair, arising from the use of a small trout fly, just one of those unaccountable freaks of fishing – or had we been fishing far too big for days?

These were events of an early April day in Donegal and recalling them has brought – and how often this happens to a fisherman – a memory of another exceptional fish from the same scene. It has a usefulness here because it demonstrates how one can contrive to defeat what can be the curse of early spring fishing in that part of the world, the north wind, synonymous curiously enough in the old Irish tongue with evil. Now the north wind, whilst not in general terms a kind wind, can suit some places provided it has a short reach to the fishing ground or provided that ground is not shallow. Where, however, the water to be fished is shallow the big waves that build up with the usually steady and usually strong north wind along or across a big lough will stir up the bottom silt and make fishing useless. I must qualify this and say that fine gritty silt in suspension matters less than vegetable debris which will sicken fish much as peat washings do. Reed beds, for example, will litter the bottom with decayed fragments and this stuff will lift with a rolling wave and put fish off.

I once struck a bad spell of north wind weather in this same lough. Day after day, that unmentionable wind sprang up about 10 a.m. and blew steadily; big rollers seethed through the reeds and the water was thick. At sunset the wind dropped, temperature fell sharply, and we had a cold clear night. By morning the stirred-up dirt of the previous day had settled along with the cooled upper layers of water. Why not, one would say, go out early before the wind of the day came up? Well, as you shall hear, that move got me one fish and cheated the north wind, and faced with similar conditions I should try this again. But fish do not move much before, say, 11 a.m. in early April unless there is an exceptionally warm air and an early start normally gains one nothing at all. Also, the north wind comes up so quickly that the interval between the development from calm to a fishing wave and thence to a big mud-stirring wave is so very short as to make such early ventures very remote chances indeed.

However, one morning, sick of watching a muddy lough and a cold green northerly sky, I did go out early and was fishing by nine-thirty in a little ripple – from the north of course. The lough was dead, apart from the odd plunging fish in the distance and for half-an-hour I tried very hard to bring a fish up to the fly. Then, true to form, at just ten o'clock the wind grew steadily from the far end of the lough and the wave built up and John kept slicing an oar and studying the water colour across the blade. He was turning the boat to pull for home when I hooked a fish among some scattered reeds – the outliers of a big bed. He had to come out of there because, apart from the hazard of the reeds where a caught-up dropper would lose us a fish, we now had the usual gale. John held the boat and I held the fish. I held him harder than I ever held a fish before and literally dragged him to the boat. He was a strong fish but I bent the old rod till it squeaked, and the tackle held and willy-nilly he came out of the reeds and presently within gaffing distance. He was neither ready nor well-placed but John clipped him cleverly and we had him – two minutes from hooking. Then everything seemed to happen at once. Untired and strong, that fish was off the gaff and crashing about the boat before the priest could be grabbed but eventually he was subdued and we could pull upwind and home with two at the oars. We had cheated the wind and we had heard a sound new to both – the squeak of a tortured rod. The fish was short and thick and fourteen pounds and by his build we knew him for a stranger – a wanderer from a neighbouring system.

I had gone to the Hebrides to catch brown trout which take well in the islands in an average June. The fish are plentiful – too plentiful – and consequently usually small but there are some lochs with a surprisingly good average weight, when one considers the type of water, overall scarcity of insect and molluscan life and the very short season when airborne food is (relatively) plentiful. The innumerable little dhu lochs on the moors are full of little black trout but there is an intermediate class, rather larger lochs as a rule, which will yield what on the mainland we used to call 'herring-size' fish and then there are a few in which trout may average just a little better than three-quarters of a pound with the odd big fish – very hard to find – running to five pounds or more.

There are, of course, a few places in the long island where there is an early run of salmon and a few sea trout but July and August are the months and a June visit is too early for migratory fish. One goes, as I had gone on this occasion, with the determination to fish for brownies. I can be very happy with a little rod and light tackle in a boat on a loch full of trout and I recall with gratitude some glorious days of Hebridean June weather doing just that.

First, however, it has to be explained that the principal scene of operations was a big irregularly shaped and rock-filled loch at the head of a long chain of others in typical island disarray. Short connecting rivers in late summer brought salmon and sea trout in from the tide. It needed big water to bring them to the top of the chain though by October the bulk of the salmon would be there. The loch is bejewelled with islets and abounds in gravelly shallows and sandy bays, but in all the miles of shoreline there are only three small patches of weed. Trout vary widely in coloration and condition – those from the dark soft peaty shores match their background, those from the commoner clean stony areas are well-conditioned, shapely and golden of belly. They are free if spasmodic risers and persistent fishing could produce very big bags. My best has been sixty-one trout for a day beginning at noon and ending in early evening and I think a full day in the right conditions could yield a hundred. Of course, it is the practice to kill only the best of the fish.

The day I remember so very well began with a three-mile tramp up and over a high ridge and down to a long straggling shallow loch, to be traversed by boat. Then, that boat drawn up again, over an area of peat gullies and old deep heather to final embarkation point. It was bright and warm with a brisk southerly breeze and a few soft clouds to give us a changing light. I had Angus for ghillie and he is one of the two best I have ever fished with, a very light nine-foot rod, a small reel with thirty yards of casting line, a little backing and a 6 lb cast with Invicta on the tail, Watson's Fancy on the dropper and Butcher on the bob. To judge from the water-level ridge on the sands by the boat, the loch had lately been a foot higher.

Trout began to move as soon as we were out of the calm lee of the higher ground and we drifted at precisely the right speed across the bay. The water sparkled, a pair of red-throated divers watched us intently from a safe distance and cloud shadows chased across the green of new spring grass on nearby hills. The colours dimmed as the hills receded until the tips of the Skye hills were the faintest of blue battlements on the far horizon. We had the beginnings of a basket of trout by the time we drifted into deeper water and they ceased to rise. Close to shore again every little shallow point produced a fish or two; we kept only those approaching the pound. There was a crisp little wave that glinted in the sun and the Butcher on the bob exactly suited conditions. Angus has little patience with trout fishing but even he sat happily in the sun while I fished the flies very fast across small waves and got enough eager rises in return to keep us interested in fishing.

Where the bay opened into the main body of the loch was a long spit of stones and we pulled out from there to cover this very good shallow strip in about four feet of water. One good trout came from the bay side of the spit and then two small nuisances as we crossed what should have been the best water. And here, to my surprise and

Angus' delight, a salmon appeared in a quick flashing interception of the tripping Butcher. If I had not seen the bright gleam of the fish as he went down I should have taken him for one of the big trout – on an even keel he looked brown and boldly spotted. 'If he makes a long run, we're done,' I said – 'so we had better be very gentle with him. If we get him we'll make history.' Salmon are not taken in that loch in June. Gentle we were, Angus creeping out from shore to safe depth while I held the fish firmly but not hard, on a fixed length of line. He went steadily out into the bay with no attempt to run or jump and there began to circle. It took twenty minutes to get him up but the unvarying firm hold did it and he came smoothly to the net without a head shake or a lash – perfectly fresh and about eight pounds. The first salmon ever to come from that loch in June.

There might be others on the spit off the headland, so while I looked out a heavier cast we went back. I changed the cast to one of 7 lbs and increased the fly size to nine, eliminating the middle fly at the same time. The trout were not put off by the heavier cast and this time over we had two keepable fish but our salmon appeared to be the only one in that particular lie. Oddly enough, even when later in the season there are many salmon, that place is not a recognized lie. We concluded, however, that if as it seemed, high water had brought in some salmon it would pay us to fish some of the known lies and forget about our trouting. I longed for a rod with rather more power and a reel with ample line and backing. There is nothing like fishing with confidence and I dreaded the smash that would certainly result if we hooked one of the wild fish that make prodigious runs, taking too much line before the boat picks up speed. It is true that one kills them sooner but thirty yards of line is grossly inadequate for fish that commonly make sixty- to eighty-yard dashes along an unobstructed loch floor and finish that with a swift upsurge and a somersault in flying spray.

We tried a good beat behind a high heather-covered island and drew a blank. A narrow rill of alkaline water came down the mountain and into the loch here, and the stony bottom was dark with moss growth, the trout were dark but shapely and well-grown. Over lunch on the pebbles of the island beach we found we had eighteen, which was fair enough since latterly I had been trying to avoid hooking them. Somewhere among the rank heather and wind-stunted rowans above and behind us was a nest of vociferous young hooded crows and Angus, with a thought for his grouse and mallard eggs, made an effort to reach and destroy the nest and its contents but soon gave up. The island was a jumble of overgrown loose rocks with leg-smashing cavities and other hazards. I always know that when Angus starts to make little post-lunch excursions he is itching to be fishing again and thinks we have wasted enough time. So we collected the gear and pushed off again.

About a quarter of a mile away upwind the loch shores close in to a narrow waist by reason of long lines of rocks which reach out from both sides, one to terminate in a small green island, the other in a pile of great boulders. Between them is no more than forty yards of open water – the only passage for a boat. The rock-strewn shallows on either side probably hold salmon but are unfishable in a light breeze and downright damaging to a boat in any real salmon-fishing wave. Today we left the shallows alone, to concentrate on a few known lies on either flank of the channel entrance. We pulled into it and drifted out. The left hand side with a huge and notorious sunken boulder on the corner was fished without result but on the next drift and on the opposite corner a fish came up very quietly beside the fly, showed his shoulders and back as he did so and went down with an unhurried little wag of his tail. The Butcher had done it again.

This fish also came willingly into deep water but soon began to show an alarming tendency to go further afield so that we were soon in fast pursuit, Angus driving the boat as only he can. In heavier water we should not have had that fish because he persistently worked so far away from the boat that I had no reserve of line. At moments when he did come slightly nearer I regained line by hand drawing, clamping a finger of the rod hand on it and then getting the slack on to the reel. I dare not allow the reel's vibration to travel directly down the line for fear of stirring the fish into a burst of running. He took longer than his predecessor and when he did come to the net I thought we were fortunate to get him since he had been on far too long. This was also a fresh fish – a little heavier than the first and when he was tapped on the head and the fly passed back to me, we had a smoke and a think.

The loch still glittered in the sun and my face burned with the reflected glare. Whilst it was true that with fish moving up the loch as they obviously were, we would come across one almost anywhere, it is a big sheet of water and not all of it fishing ground. We were in a trout fishing area, the day having been so planned, and there remained of true salmon lies thereabouts, only one as yet unfished. It lies off a low peaty headland where shallow water covers a stony flat reaching out into the loch. The bottom is not as clean as I like to see it – hard patches alternating with soft ground and I have never had much faith in it which is perhaps why I have never had any success there. Angus used all his very considerable boatcraft in fishing it but we failed to move anything and having covered it moved back towards the bay entrance where we had the first fish. Another fish *might* have occupied the lie – if lie it was – but if so he did not want the Butcher or the Silver Doctor on the tail.

We ended our active fishing pulling slowly and diagonally across the bay to the boat landing while I cast a long line, more from habit than from hope, at right angles to our course and allowed the flies to swing round towards our wake. On some lakes, in the spring fishing, this will raise more fish than conventional casting. It is not so every day and I have a feeling that there is some condition of weather, wind and wave that favours the method. I have never been able to find enough constants to identify the condition and know only that it works better on a rough day than on a quiet one – but then, so do other methods.

Anyhow, that is what I was doing when Angus shipped his oars and allowed the boat to glide over the shallows to the beach. And there, in eighteen inches of crystal clear calm water over sand as flat and featureless as an area of concrete, I hooked a third fish. The boat grounded and the fish jumped. We saw he was small – I concluded I could play him from the stern with the boat where she was, but Angus pushed off ten yards to give us mobility. That little fish gave me much more trouble than either of the others. He was everywhere in short dashes and lashing jumps, stimulated probably by the very shallowness of the water. It was good clean fun until the reel retaining band, which must have been working loose for some time, slipped off the plate and the reel fell at my feet. A return from there would have been simple but the reel disappeared from sight where floorboard failed to meet stern frame. It continued to revolve, however, when I needed more line and with care to stand still so that the yards of loose line came up from the boards unchecked and by guiding payout from a light grasp on the line, the fish was played. It was by no means as difficult as it might appear although I would not care much for it with a big fish.

This one was an elegant grilse of four pounds so that we ended this day of surprises with two salmon and a grilse and twenty-one brown trout. It kept us talking all of the way back up the other loch and over the hill to home.

I was happy that evening to enter in the estate fishing records the first capture of salmon in June and doing so under the fourth of the month was prompted by some quirk of fancy to look, several volumes back, at results of other anglers on other fourths in earlier years.

The entry for the fourth of August 1914 read: 'War declared on Germany. Wind went south in afternoon.'

Flies of the Wild Shore

One of the discoveries which every keen fisherman for
salmon and sea trout makes as a long succession of seasons
passes by is how few patterns of flies are really necessary
for the waters he fishes. Naturally, if he is fortunate
enough to be able to range far and wide on rivers and
lakes from the far north of Scotland to the Islands, to
Donegal and Connemara and Kerry and back to Wales
and the West Country, he will need many fly boxes to
house his bare requirements. But for each individual
fishing the variety of flies will be small, and since most
men have favourite waters or places where they enjoy
some rights or privileges of fishing, the accumulation of
vast ranges of patterns does not arise of necessity. It may
and usually does arise from other causes, and every
devoted angler has scores of flies that he never or very
seldom uses – flies bought on someone's recommendation
– on the strength of one good day with some special
pattern – or in conformity with local fancy. It is an
expensive and rather silly practice and I am as foolish as
anyone. Every so often I have a clearing-out but I lack the
courage (or the heart) to discard from hundreds of flies I
shall never use, beautifully tied, new-conditioned dressings bought at some time as being absolutely 'the' fly for
such and such a water. The trouble is that I did not buy

three and try the fly – I bought a dozen and still have
eleven of them – bright, attractive in their way, and
useless.

There is another difficulty in the way of being hard-
hearted and sensible in keeping the numbers of patterns
down and that is the fact that 'odd' patterns do sometimes
kill fish. Whether they are established local dressings or
just someone's experiments does not matter and because
they once served well, they will be retained with a certain
affection.

There is little point in an attempt to define a short
standard range of patterns for general use. To do so with
any usefulness to the individual one has to know where
the bulk of his fishing is done. The fly that will take
salmon anywhere *may* exist and if it does will be found in
my opinion among Yellow Torrish, Thunder and Lightning, Dusty Miller, Black Doctor and Silver Grey. A
range, in assorted sizes, for the man who fishes usually in
one river or lough somewhere in these islands might be
these flies plus local patterns – or other standard dressings
which kill well locally because they suit water colour or
for some undissectable reason. Perhaps – and it is a highly
gratifying phenomenon – the fish just like them.

Thus acknowledging the problem presented by the all-
purpose, all-locality standard range, I must say that I have
found a few flies devised to meet purely local 'tastes'
which seem to have some general usefulness within my
own experience. That there are many of these which are
sea trout patterns is odd, because the laying-down of a
standard sea trout range is a much simpler matter than is
the case with salmon flies – the basic dressings usually
being acceptable to sea trout in spite of the multiplicity of
variations and purely local fancies. A fly box containing
Butcher, Mallard and Claret, Woodcock or Mallard and

Yellow, Blue and Silver, Zulu, Blue Zulu, Connemara Black and Peter Ross in assorted sizes would equip me to fish wet fly confidently anywhere. On the basis of sound and tested local information I should probably add the river or loch special particularly if I were night fishing.

This business of fly dressings, hook sizes and shapes is probably as productive of amiable wrangling among fishermen as any of the fishing subjects which abound in ifs and buts, exceptions and reservations. Someone will pick a fly from someone else's fly box and say, 'What do you call that?' 'That? oh, that's a Green Imp – Brora fly you know. Funny thing, they won't have it without the guineafowl. I remember . . .' And then it starts. Another man says, 'Down on the So-and-so in Kerry we always use a Coiner with a dark hackle. I was there one day and the river was a bit coloured . . .' More fly boxes are produced and more tales of super critical fish are told. Ours is a happy pastime.

I must go back now to the question of suitable patterns of salmon flies for special conditions, to be added to the standard range of your fancy and your need. To Lemon Grey for misty weather and filtered light, Dusty Miller (primarily as a dropper in lough fishing) for bright weather and Fiery Brown for high peat-stained flood water I will add two for dark overcast days and very rough water and two for similar conditions but quieter water. The first pair consist of Black Fairy, an Irish pattern of general usefulness on days as sombre as the dressing – which is for all practical purposes a Mallard and Black with black hackle, and another Irishman, the Claret. All that need be added in respect of the Black Fairy is that the wool body should be roughly teased out between the turns of gold tinsel. The Claret, not often seen nowadays, is dressed with dark mallard wings and a few long fibres

of jay. The body is made up of a sparsely wound bur-
gundy-coloured hackle overlaid with four or five turns of
flat gold tinsel. There can be, but need not be, a butt of
black herl and the tail is a few golden whisks. Hackle is
jay mixed with the first few turns of the burgundy body
hackle. This fly, providing the body winding has the true
prismatic quality, glows like a dark jewel even in bad
light. It will, like Fiery Brown, do well in peat-stained
water. The other pair, doing better as already noted in
quieter water, possibly because of their better entry are
Thunder and Lightning and Sweep. Both are standard
patterns and require no description and both are bad light
flies. Sweep, indeed, often fishes well in darkness if you
have a mind to try for a salmon so late in the day. As an
after-sunset fly when salmon may be moving but the light
has not yet quite gone, it can be excellent. I have done
well with it in the throats of river pools when the fish
have been taking their evening cruise, and in the current
where a river enters the lough. It seems to do best in sizes
not larger than six. In reasonably broken but not turbulent
water I should fish an eight. I think perhaps that to my
dark weather list I should add Black Doctor, a fly most
effective in the Hebrides so long as it is fished in small
sizes. I have had many salmon on sizes as small as ten but
I have only once taken a fish on a size over eight.

Golden Olive, again an Irish pattern, has been serving
me rather well in recent years for both salmon and sea
trout – the salmon mainly in Ireland and on loughs, and
the sea trout pretty generally. The yellow wool body
shows up well and the fly almost always *looks* right in a
variety of lights. In one lough I know where salmon show
a decided preference for light-coloured flies predominantly
yellow in tone I would rate Golden Olive and Yellow
Torrish as equal best. But, fishing both on the cast as I

often do, I like the Olive, which has more weight when wet, to be the uppermost of the two because a bulky-bodied dropper tripping rather better brings up more fish than a clean-lined fly creating less surface distortion. It may be a fine point but fishing is full of them.

The Olive can readily replace Mallard and Yellow in the standard sea trout range as the differences are small. My own choice is the Olive which I carry in small sizes for summer salmon anyhow, and therefore have the fly in sizes suitable for sea trout whenever I wish to include it on a cast. While we are in the homeland of the golden fly I ought to list Connemara Black which seems to be more widely known and appreciated than formerly. Thirty years ago it was hardly seen outside the west of Ireland but now it is often seen in Scotland. There are few really dark sea trout flies – one thinks off hand only of Butcher, Zulu and Black Pennell, and Connemara Black fills a gap in that among dark flies it simulates the natural fly more closely than others.

If we exclude the unquestionable truth that certain patterns, especially in salmon flies, will take fish to the near exclusion of others in specific areas, it is simple and sensible to argue that one should cut the range down to, say, ten patterns and a limited number of sizes in each, and this advice has been tendered so often that there is little point in my listing any such chosen ten. My choice of at least half of them will not agree with another man's short list – so much depends on the type or location of water which has provided most of one's experience, and upon one's way of fishing – so that we go on and on and before long are back into a multiplicity of patterns to meet a variety of theoretical needs.

Now, quite apart from the considerations which prompt one's adherence to a short list, or, on the other hand, to an expanded and heterogeneous one, I am suggesting that there is a special list which can be carried to meet specific needs arising from fishing conditions rather than from situation or locality. It is a very short range indeed, but rather than list it for you I propose to describe sundry combinations of wind, weather, water and light, and temperature which we fishermen usefully call 'conditions'. For each of these I will suggest a basic fly and if some of these suit conditions which occur with some frequency, then one has a pattern for inclusion in a true short list if you happen to believe in the principle of an all-purpose short range.

Consider then, and for a first example, the condition which arises when we have an east wind, commonly and rightly regarded as a plague. East wind effects can vary with locality and topography but none are good. In the early part of the year this wind can be cuttingly cold, lowering water temperature and putting fish down, and later on in the season we are apt to get in place of the cold a very bad light, hazy and dim, not quite leaden but having the same lifeless quality. Neither sea trout nor salmon will move, and the trouble is that this kind of weather will often persist for days with the fish daily becoming stiffer, if that is possible. I know of no fly particularly calculated to interest salmon in dull east wind conditions, but the simple Teal and Red for sea trout is peculiarly attractive and I always use it. Others to whom I have made this comment have equal faith after trying it, and only this season an acquaintance whom I hadn't encountered for some years said, when we met by chance in Scotland, 'I'll always be grateful for a tip you once gave me – to fish Teal and Red in an east wind. I always do and I find it works.' He did not know why any more than I do. My faith in it was founded in early days in Scotland when I used to fish in early March as soon as the season opened, on high lochs where the east wind cut like a knife across open moors. One day, by chance, I fished Teal and Red and made a big bag of good trout and repeated it the next day and the next again. After that I really began to take note and, whilst I cannot say that I have never known it to fail, there has been nothing to shake my early faith in this fly. So here is one for the special range – Teal and Red for trout and sea trout in east wind conditions.

Sea trout sometimes take very well in moderate rain and there is one Irish ghillie I know who maintains stoutly that salmon like the kind of rain that makes holes in the lake. He has been demonstrably right about this too, but for proof I would like to see the theory working out when all other conditions were unfavourable. Trout will take freely in warm rain up to moderate weight if you can find something to please them. I have a fly which takes both sea trout and trout in rain so well that I call it the 'Rain Fly', and I am never without it.

I came on the prototype by chance. Looking idly over the contents of an antique/junk shop window in a little West Country town one day, I saw a small heap of fly boxes looking curiously out of place among candlesticks and horse-brasses. I bought them with their contents for a few shillings. Where the former owner had fished I could not guess, so many of the flies were to me quaint and anonymous – among them the Rain Fly. Here is the dressing. The head immediately behind the eye is built up into bulbous shape with black tying silk and takes up a third of the shank of the hook. Then come a couple of turns of creamy white hackle, rather long, and the remaining two-thirds of the body are sparsely wound black chenille. There is no tail or tag. The finished fly looks like a dark beetle with light legs and wing cases and fishes best on the bob, because the chenille holds air and the fly has a bad entry. It is conceivable that this may be a local pattern or an old-time standard pattern but I have never seen it described or illustrated during the twenty-five years or so I have been using it. It will only succeed, by the way, in small sizes.

From rain I turn to mist and to salmon, and I think if I were asked to name the condition least favourable for salmon fishing I should say mist – low-hanging mist – the kind that clings to the hillsides and produces such a 'keeping down' effect on the fish even when it lingers only on the higher slopes. How often do you hear a ghillie say 'We'll do no good till that mist lifts off the hill', and he is making good use of his local knowledge and is right. He possibly doesn't know it but he would be just as right in his assessment of the chances anywhere else, because mist of any degree is bad everywhere. I can never be quite sure whether the barometric condition of which the mist is the indicator is affecting the fish, or whether it is the effect of the mist on the light. The latter cannot be the case where mist lingers on the tops only, but it can be, and I am quite certain is, where mist is low-hanging and light consequently filtered and poor.

It is this local condition that makes fish, even very fresh, difficult to move, and the one remedy in my experience is the Lemon Grey. I first discovered this in Donegal in the early thirties and nothing I have seen since has shaken my confidence in this beautiful fly. There should be the air of 'rightness' which the fly must carry as you swim it experimentally before fishing. If you try the Lemon Grey on one of these misty days you will see that in most waters without suspended dirt it looks right. But here there is need for a word of caution or reservation. I often see factory-tied flies labelled Lemon Grey which are in my opinion quite useless lumpy fabrications of grey wool. The grey of the body foundation must be light and not lumpy, just lightly picked out, and showing the tinsel clearly. The hackle should be bright and prismatic and sparse. So dressed, this fly, in the conditions for which it is devised, is absolutely right and looks it. Irish dressers generally make a better job of it than others, possibly because they are working with traditional materials with which the best of them have outstanding skill.

Similar skill is vital to the make-up of a good Fiery Brown, my fourth special condition fly. This is a very old Irish fly, well known in its country of origin, but not fished enough in the water it suits best, either in Ireland or Scotland. I seem to see it and hear it mentioned oftener in recent years in Scotland and perhaps there is a growing appreciation of its usefulness, but I rarely see what I consider to be a proper dressing. The real true old dressing has a body colour exceedingly hard to describe. It is a very dark glowing ginger-brown – not the strident ginger that has a hint of orange in its make-up, but the hot brown of snow-flattened dead bracken. The body is wool with about five turns of wide gold tinsel and with the wool picked out between the turns; tail is a whisk of golden pheasant. Wings are dark mallard and not too heavy. Some tyers include horns of tippet or a few fibres of blue macaw, but I doubt the necessity for these. Hackle matches the body colour, but an old man in Killarney who used to produce the most lovely Irish patterns for me, always incorporated a few fibres of sparkling yellow in the hackle, following the custom now almost gone, of achieving a general effect by mixing materials. The result had life and sparkle and exceptionally good light transmission. The wings of commercially produced Fiery Browns are usually acceptable but I have seen bodies varying in colour from offensive light orangy ginger to yellows like the body of a Golden Olive. These don't look right either in the hand or in the water.

Fiery Brown is pre-eminently a peat water fly and one for big and coloured waters in that category. Perhaps because of this it will fish successfully in bigger sizes than one would use in other patterns in similar conditions, and I have had many lake fish, in spring particularly, on fours and even twos. My suggestion that the fly is best in peat water is based on its failure, with me as with others, when used in the West Country, in Wales or in lowland waters generally. In short, it is a fly for highland rivers and lakes when they go wine-dark in spate conditions and the moorland flotsam gathers in the eddies.

Whilst I have been putting these thoughts on paper I have been repeatedly side-tracked by recollections of notable days with other flies – days when a particular fly seemed to be the only thing that would move fish – cold days and hot ones – days when the water looked opaque or unnaturally clear, and days when I seemed to be on the verge of a great discovery. Such days dance, in fact and in memory, like a fisherman's will o' the wisp and share all its lack of substance and permanence. All they do is to fill the fly box with dressings that never kill again and lead to the very thing which with my very short special list I am trying to prevent. So I have restrained myself from writing too much about the Claret, salmon fly supreme in some places, and the Golden Olive, the Green Highlander and Hairy Mary. These belong to a standard list – not in that related to specific conditions.

Wrenched, with great effort I freely admit, from this sort of contemplation and this sort of confusing advice to you, I turn now with resolution to another special – Dusty Miller. This dressing is too well known and, on the whole, well executed to need description, and in this connection I will only say that I call a Dusty Miller, affectionately, 'The Dusty', by this name when it has the true pinky-flame hackle. I do not like and I do not recommend the grey-hackled version so often seen. Another variant has a lime-green hackle and it was responsible for the downfall of the first salmon I ever caught in the West of England; like the one-occasion killer already referred to, it has never tempted another fish – though it has often tempted me. So the pink-hackled Dusty is the one and for a bright day with continuous sun, or only blinks of it – it has, by my standard, no equal. This is the sunny day fly and although I have used it successfully in Norway in 4/o's and bigger it does best at home in small sizes from six downwards and works best, exploiting broken and good light, on the bob. I always fish two flies for salmon in lakes and I calculate, and the diary proves, that seventy-five per cent of my fish are caught on the dropper. In bright weather that dropper is always the 'Dusty' and whilst I list it as a fly for this common but sometimes difficult condition, I also consider that it has a double entitlement to inclusion in the range, because it is a good standard pattern for a fairly wide assortment of conditions and it will take fish anywhere that I have ever fished.

I have no record of the true dressing of the Donegal Blue and I have never seen or heard of one differing in any way from those I have fished for some years. It's a fly with, in suitable conditions, a kind of magic in it. Salmon, sea trout and brown trout take it avidly in a reasonable range of water colours and heights and I have seen salmon slash savagely at it even on a blue day. On such a day it has something of the quality of the Blue-bottle though this latter has more attraction for sea trout than for salmon. A blue day, I should add, is the day with a brisk but not necessarily strong breeze when the wave hollows reflect the intense blue of a cloud-free area of sky. I do not like a day of clear cloudless sky and intense blue water. There *are* places where it seems to suit, but infinitely more which it decidedly does not.

The dressing with which I am both familiar and markedly successful is very simple. Body is coarse wool of a rather faded medium blue overlaid by a few turns of broad silver tinsel. There are no wings but there is a head hackle of black hen fibres. I don't think the source is important so long as the hackle is soft and of medium length. The fly fishes best on the bob, less well on the dropper and seldom on the tail. I will, however, qualify the last dictum by saying that it will fish on the tail as a Black Pennell occasionally will on quiet days when a deep slow fly seems to provoke the only takes. But I would never make up a cast with the blue fly so placed, choosing rather to change an existing cast layout by putting it on the tail if wind falls too light – or in conditions of drizzly calm. When the wool body is thoroughly saturated the fly will fish deep on a slow retrieve.

I shall, however, assuredly be taken to task if I suggest persistent fishing for sea trout in calm conditions – and certainly by those habitually fishing small lakes, lochs or loughs. In a big water the choice of ground is so extensive that the point has little weight but it is true beyond any shadow of doubt that persistent calm fishing – however cautiously carried out – will put sea trout 'off' where the loch is small and the area limited. I've seen this happen, the fish going down just as salmon will if repeatedly trolled or spun over. Not nearly enough attention is paid to the inbuilt shyness of sea trout. In fact this fish has an undeserved reputation for boldness because of the dash and freedom of his taking when fresh from the sea. But no fish learns more quickly and once the first freshness is off, sea trout heavily fished will not look at the fly – I mean *any* fly – except on the odd days when even the dark fish, weeks or even months in the lake, come 'on'. The great trouble then is that the take comes on without warning at any hour and may last a quarter or half an hour – or perhaps minutes only.

The ways of sea trout are of such extraordinary interest that I've been led away from my Donegal Blue and I return to it now and especially to the blueness of it, for that is the key to its success. When I first fished it – on the bob – I thought that it functioned as a Black Pennell, a plain Black Spider or a smallish Zulu would in a suitable wave. At a glance there is not a great deal of difference between one hackled black fly and another: if suitably dressed the hackles of all will work well – dipping in the wave and working like the legs of a swimming or strug-gling insect and for those reasons alone bringing up fish. But this is not so.

I have repeatedly fished all of these flies with indifferent success on certain days and begun to bring up fish after fish to the Donegal Blue as soon as I changed the bob fly. Salmon will certainly come to the Zulu in good wave conditions but in my experience seldom take it. They are drawn to the disturbance of the surface caused by the bad entry of the Zulu but in the main turn away. Not so with the Blue – and they will take it fiercely and well, oftener in small sizes than in those larger than nines. Admittedly I do regularly fish lochs where small sizes in any pattern will do better than large versions and I have not given the Donegal Blue in large sizes any sort of extensive trial – an

omission which robs this account of a single fly's attrac-
tiveness of any claim to being a piece of research. Most
lochs will yield better results anyhow if the fly size is kept
down and at risk of wearying readers on whom my views
have been inflicted I will assert again that most people fish
too big. I would not fish the blue fly or any other in a big
wave in size ten, which is too small for rough conditions,
but that size is standard with me for most days of small or
medium wave. Salmon see it well and take it and sea trout
do so in all states of wind and water as do brown trout.
Their preference for it in most places, not alone in the
Irish county of its name can be astonishing. I have
repeatedly used patterns like Butcher, Mallard and Yellow
(or Golden Olive) and Mallard and Claret on the cast with
it – to have them ignored and sea trout after sea trout
came avidly after the blue fly on the bob.

There can be unaccountable runs of luck in all fishing
and there is too, always the possibility that a killing fly
may be fished by its owner in a specially attractive manner
with the result that it is less effective when fished by
someone else in *his* style. And again – there is that strange
circumstance in which one rod of a pair in a straight
drifting boat rises fish after fish while the other does not.
I have checked and double-checked all these possibilities
in their possible relation to my blue with the help of a
companion rod and have found that the man fishing the
blue was the man raising and getting the fish – quite
irrespective of his position in the boat or of his style of
working the fly. A novice fishing the blue will raise more
fish than a skilful angler applying all his knowledge and
dexterity to the working of another pattern. And if you
think that is putting it a bit high – put it to the test.

There can be little doubt of the sea trout's liking for
blue either as the overall general hue in a fly, or as an

element in the dressing. As witness take the Donegal Blue's conventional near equivalent – Bluebottle. Dressings for this vary considerably. Some have slim dark blue bodies consisting of a light winding of dark silk while others – especially in Ireland – have plump bodies of bright blue chenille. I like these latter for lough fishing but the slimmer bodied types for river work. Blue Zulu, most widely used in the Scottish north-west, in my experience is curiously patchy in its appeal and I do not myself fish it outside that area with any real confidence. But it does do very well indeed in some places – it's the bluest of all flies and sea trout like it.

There can be no argument about the merits of dry fly in a calm or in that tiny surface crinkle which is nearly as bad. Often a very good class of sea trout will come to a small Black Pennell put down softly and left sitting out as far from boat or bank as one can conveniently get it. A biggish high-riding fly works well in a lively wave too.

Equally there can be no doubt about the effectiveness of the dap on a rough day of steady breeze because it surely has no equal as an attractor of big sea trout. On the right day the dap will always, in my experience, produce a better class of fish, often from deep water, than either conventional dry fly – hardly suitable for such conditions – or the wet fly which is in every way suitable. But if the dap scores in size the wet fly, properly fished, will take the greater number. Of course, with the requisite skill and versatility one will suit the method to the day, but it seems to me that dapping is regarded too often as a mystique whose devotees have an almost total disregard for the older methods; they look particularly askance at wet fly. I admit – I have already done so – the attraction of the dap for big sea trout; some of the best ever to be caught in our lakes have been so taken but I contend that wet fly, properly fished, will month by month and over the season beat the dap in numbers and perhaps in gross weight. It is a subject often and hotly argued. My own pleasure in occasional dapping is beside the point. I enjoy an odd day with the big light rod and the, to me, somewhat intractable running tackle, but there for me it ends, though I am far from disdaining the method because I like it less than regular wet fly.

Granted a breeze of some sort, and a wave above the merest crinkle, there are no days when wet fly cannot be fished but there are many days when the dap is out of place because wind and wave are not quite good enough; but the confirmed dappers are out. Their faith in the dap, and it has its rather strong fascination, is clearly greater than in the older method.

Would it be so, one wonders, if they fished wet and exploited the attraction of the bob as it should be used. They would not tempt as many big fish and they would not bring so many up from deep water but if sea trout are in any sort of taking mood the fast-tripping bob will bring them up. The problem of how to hook the fish that slashes at a fast bob is no greater than that presented by a deliberate take on the dap. Whether the conception of the bob and dropper was based on the desire to fish as many flies as possible, or whether it was designed to provide a surface-fishing fly as well as one or several sunk lures on one and the same cast, I do not really know. I suspect that numbers of flies were originally used quite simply to provide more chances of attracting fish by showing a variety of patterns. As a boy I fished on the lovely Clyde in its mid and upper reaches and on that beautiful trout river I remember being shown the casts, some horsehair, of the very skilful miner anglers who came from the Lanarkshire towns. They fished eight or ten flies to a cast *and* in the dusk. It is a sobering reflection for those of us who find three flies troublesome enough in a dark night's sea trout fishing.

I have an idea that a cast of three flies on the loch and for sea trout means to many men the opportunity to fish three contrasting patterns and not, as it should be, a means whereby they may present the flies in two different ways with the patterns chosen by shape, size and colour to suit those ways.

The tail fly and if there are three on the cast, the dropper fly, should fish under the surface, how far under depending on speed of recovery. The bob should fish on the surface and it should trail at its chosen speed – properly rather fast – leaving a little wake or furrow and tripping from wave to wave. And by the way, though I am now speaking of sea trout, the bob action should be used for salmon though the speed of working is of course much slower. Loch salmon, if they move at all, will come freely to a lively bob action in a rough wave. Method of line recovery is simpler with the slower fly.

For fast fishing for sea trout the means of line recovery is all-important because, of course, it regulates the speed of the fly and there are three ways of doing this. First and used too widely, involves casting just as much line off the reel as is easy with whatever rod is in use. Whether a loop of line is held in the left hand or not, this procedure dictates fly recovery by rod motion alone and is far too inflexible and can be tiring. Second, seen oftener in the south than the north, is the technique in which some extra yards of line are shot in the forward cast and recovered by wrist action which turns the left hand one way and then the other while the fingers gather line into the palm of the hand. The rod meanwhile moves very little. One can fish very fast indeed this way but only the most practised with a tireless left-hand action can keep it up throughout a long day. It also calls for the most disciplined reaction to a rise because the rod is stationary and has at the instant stimulus of a rise to go into action as it were from scratch.

Far preferable is the trick of using both hand recovery and rod motion. Throw some, perhaps three or four yards of extra line, adjusting length of line in relation to rod-length and your height above the water in such a way that the bob fly is on the surface as soon as possible after recovery begins. Then the fly can be kept tripping the surface at whatever speed one wants by hand-lining plus backward movement of the rod to the vertical. I prefer to coil line into my left hand with the fingers of that hand, because I do not like dropping loose line into the boat or on the bank. Line can be dropped by the stern rod in a boat; he usually has a flat obstruction-free floor beneath him but in the bow there are often the ends of floor slats which have a devilish attraction for loops of line. And if a big one takes hold while line is hooked up there is surely trouble. Ashore it may easily be even worse; if line does not become snagged by twigs or bulbous-headed rushes it either picks up grit or falling in the water becomes sodden and will not shoot as it should. The business of gathering some yards of line in the palm of the hand may seem laborious or even complicated but it is not and anyone with normally flexible fingers can learn it quickly.

It is clear, I think, that line-gathering and rod movement together provide the greatest possible versatility in fly-working. Speed is infinitely variable and direction across or along the wave to some extent with it. You can also on occasion cover a rising fish by release of a few yards of line without having to tear it hastily off the reel. Some fishermen do not like having yards of line in the hand when a fish is hooked, preferring to have the fish playing off the reel as soon as hooked. This is sound enough but I have never found any difficulty in feeding the gathered-up line to the fish through my fingers and in getting him, in seconds, on to the reel.

The tripped fly has two functions: one to attract to itself, the other to the following tail fly, or to dropper and tail; therefore, the top fly must be of the attractor class and it need not look at all like any nymph or any winged fly. Usually it should have flash or colour or both. I believe the best bob fly of all for sea trout is the Butcher; but a Peter Ross, Teal and Red, Blue and Silver or a small Silver Doctor will do well in most places.

There is, however, another type of attractor which does well in certain conditions – in my experience usually in rough water – and that is the Zulu, either the usual black, silver ribbing and red tag dressing, or the blue version – curiously local in usefulness – or the Red Palmer. Zulu is extraordinarily killing sometimes, fished tripping the sur-face and making a distinct wake. In rough conditions, it makes a better 'disturbance' than the less bushy patterns which have a better entry.

Wet fly fished this way is, unquestionably, the most effective method on most days throughout the season. Keep the dapping rod and the shaving brushes for the days that suit them best.

In between the rough days when the sea trout take the wet fly well and the weather is what Michael calls 'a bit coarse', I like a warm sunny day with a light breeze and for tools a lightish rod and a line to suit. And because there comes a time anyhow when the sea trout suddenly go off and the bag is unlikely to contain anything other than finnock, I use a dry fly of the type which dapping experience shows will bring up the bigger fish which wet fly will not. But dapping again is for the rougher days and I'm thinking of a method which is best used in a wind and wave far too light for the dap yet strong enough for the nearly futile wet fly. In big rough rivers or very small ones sea trout lie thickest in the big pools, flats and dead-looking water and much that one would ignore in fishing for browns or salmon will turn out to be the best so long as you have a breeze. With the Loch Ordie you can seek out the best class of sea trout. Most of my fishing calls for boat and ghillie but I have had equal success on certain of the long dead stretches of canal-like water on some western Scottish and Irish mountain rivers which lose life and movement once they come down off the steeper slopes and meander sluggishly across the moor or the coastal flat.

The great thing about a day with a floating fly that requires the minimum of casting or false casting, as distinct from traditional dry fly, is that you can be still: you see and learn much that is, of necessity, unobserved when you are pre-occupied with a more active technique. But you can judge if I tell you about a day that was reasonably and fairly typical.

My lough runs north and south on the west coast of Ireland and is preserved water carefully fished and seldom flogged but dour which merely emphasizes the utter unresponsiveness even of undisturbed sea trout in some of their humours. Four miles of rough river connect it to the sea and every tide will bring many fresh sea trout and a few grilse or summer salmon from the beginning of July to the end of August. There is unlimited variety of shoreline and many islands and islets and a clean gravel, sand or boulder-strewn bottom almost everywhere. The water is amber tinted – but clear. There are sheltered bays guarded by piled glacial boulders and inlets where little rivers chuckle through dense mossy woods to lose themselves over golden sand offshore. There are very quiet bays too, where guardian headlands take the thrust of prevailing wind to shield acres of giant reeds from all but the residual surge of waves from round the corner. And on the shore, under downswept hazel and alder the pale primrose green of the royal fern growing in dignity among aged rocks at the margin of lapping water. Sandy or pebbly beaches line some shores and everywhere beyond and above woodcock-haunted woodlands and thickets of holly, the mountains show, the soft blue of them like the bloom on the ripe sloe.

There is one shallow reedy bay which however thin the sea trout run of the moment may be, always holds fish. It has everything that sea trout like – a string of rocky islets, clean hard ground, ample feed from three little entering rivers, and shelter in dense reeds always close. Here in mid-morning on a pleasant early July day you would have found Michael and me – objective to try to move some of the big sea trout. We had arrived with a slight inferiority complex because, rounding the point to enter the bay, we had been tempted to try a drift with the wet fly outfit of yesterday. So doing, we had risen, hooked and played a fresh grilse that had, as Michael said 'the divvle in him' for he twisted and turned and contorted his slim body as though he were made of wire springs and, having by this means enlarged the hook hold, jumped and threw the hook. However lightly I held the fish made no difference nor lessened his mad gyrations – he might have been hooked in the tongue but in that case I would not have expected him to come off so readily. However this might be, the accident had taken, as I say, the edge off our self-esteem when the boat lost way and began to drift broad-side in the light breeze away from the edge of the reeds. As soon as I was clear in the backcast of the six-foot plumes behind me I put out a medium-sized Loch Ordie.

The fly consists of two palmer-like bodies in tandem – single hooks on each and sometimes a tiny flying triangle suspended from the leading body. The pattern I chose had dense hackles of dark furnace red the length of each body, but showing a glint of gold tinsel and each had at the head, hackles of creamy white – total length with ¼ inch gap between bodies, about 1¾ inches. Well doped and carefully handled this thing will float indefinitely and if the hackles are good will sit up beautifully looking like a big hairy caterpillar perhaps, but like nothing else that I know of.

The fly has an interesting history. It was invented and used in the United States by that great angler Edward R. Hewitt and was originally aimed at imitation of a butterfly and in size much larger than anything used here. Hewitt called it the 'Neversink Skater' and used it in Scotland when the Duke of Atholl gave him a day on Loch Ordie where, as you will guess, the fly achieved great things with the big trout for which the loch was famous. I believe that the original fly had one large hook and though I have never tried it so dressed I am sure the fly is best equipped as I have described.

The trick of fishing it is simple enough. You get out as much line as you comfortably can and put it down lightly so that the full length floats evenly and the Loch Ordie bobs erect without trace of drag at this stage. You will find that it catches the wind and will pull the line quite straight: as soon as this happens you begin to feed line slowly, smoothly by hand so that the 'fly' searches more

[134]

and more water. When the length of floating line is such that clearly you could not strike any taking fish, you recover, laying the uncastable portion of your long line on clean floorboards or seat ready to pay out again.

In this way then my Loch Ordie was fishing and the lost grilse all but forgotten and we were happy, Michael and I: the sun was shining, the southwest wind warm and gust-free and the 'fly' danced on waves of just the right height. The fish might be anywhere either close to the reeds or a hundred yards or so out where there were two piles of submerged boulders or perhaps in the channel between the aforesaid boulders and the island of gulls – you could never be sure. But today one fish at least was out in the bay for within a few minutes there was a light splash and a big boil and the fly had gone. The strike – a slow one – met a solid resistance and we at once had a jump from what was clearly a good fish. It was, when we had him in the boat he looked about three and a half pounds – well hooked on the tiny flying triangle. This was better. Michael, clearly much uplifted in spirit, began an animated argument with a small mobbing of gulls intent on driving us away from their nesting island.

The Loch Ordie, spruced up again, was put out once more but seemed to be fishing over some very shallow ground because I began to be bothered by smallish brownies. Some tried splashily to drown the fly and some would give it a tug and half drown it: eventually we moved inshore to an unfished sector of the reed bed fringe. Here we had for company a pair of feeding dabchicks, confiding little birds – bundles of warm brown without apparent fear of the boat, always busy and worth watching. They do in fact repay some attention because if you fail to keep an eye on them you may find yourself casting to a feeding sea trout only to realise when it's too late that this 'rise' was the surface disturbance following the upending of a diving dabchick. They go down with such a quick flip.

I missed the next fish to come to the Loch Ordie but could not tell whether it was a small fish finding it too big a mouthful or a good fish that took and rejected in a flash. This latter will happen although the flying triangle will usually prevent it unless the fly has not been wholly engulfed. The timing of the strike is obviously critical but it's difficult to vary with such a long line and one has infinitely less capacity for variation in timing than is possible with ordinary wet or dry fly and relatively short line.

By the time I had the fly dry and redoped and bobbing downwind again we were out in the bay area once more and slightly east of the drift which had given us our first fish. It was coming up to one o'clock of the sun and normally, if there is anything that can be said to be normal in sea trout behaviour, a good taking time, I changed tactics, putting life into the Loch Ordie. If you draw the thing gently a few inches at a time it provides an extraordinarily life-like simulation of some wind-carried 'creature' struggling on the surface film and often provokes the kind of slashing take that comes to the dap. Five minutes of this and I had a fierce rise and a line taut with a good fish making a determined run for an outlying clump of reeds on our right. This is a common trick, particularly of the larger class of fish and knowing it you try to keep the boat between fish and obstruction. Because of the line of drift dictated by wind direction for this kind of fishing we could not do it today, but I held as hard as the five pound nylon would permit, and by moving the boat obtained a degree of side-strain so that the fish cleared the lakeward end of the reeds. The taut cast bowed the few outlying growths and we were clear – a wet fly cast with droppers would almost certainly have fouled. This fish would have none of the net and twice found new strength to fight away for short runs. When we did have him aboard we judged him five pounds – a bulky thick-shouldered cock – by no means fresh but a good fish and vindication of the Loch Ordie on a day when you'd be lucky to get pounders by any other method. On the scales later we found we had over judged, misled by the heavy shoulders, and he was only four-and-a-half. But he would do and we went happily to lunch under the trees with the boat's nose aground on the gravel among the reeds.

Here to our right was an open lagoon fringed with lily beds and forests of six-foot rushes – its surface barely ruffled by the breeze. This is the nursery for the gulls and squadrons of curiously pert nestlings executed complicated paddling manoeuvres in its shelter, while hidden under the trees, we had some respite from the screaming protests of their parents. On the far shore of the lough a boat drifted by one of the stony points – the occupant's identity known to us even at that distance from his attitude at the oars.

The stern of the boat was beyond the limit of the shade and when we pushed off again I found the seat hot and sun obviously much hotter and brighter and killing the breeze. With the usually rather dead afternoon period on us, I had slight hope. There would be no shadow even in bays fringed by tall trees until evening. There was however one very good place where a day or two previously we had seen some good sea trout showing – again close to the ever-present reeds.

If we could add another fish to the bag it would be here: the boat was turned downwind and a quarter of a mile on we lay-to just inside and downwind of a long low point which ended in a gravel ridge running far into the lough.

Inside the point the reeds began again – a dense semi-circular bed off the silt-laden outflow of a small river. Big sea trout always lie hereabouts, sometimes close in and on some evenings they will show well inside the reeds and among the stems – quite unattainable of course.

Today – as happens so curiously often with these places for which hopes are high – these places that beckon you from distant drifts – we were plagued by finnock of the usual ten to twelve ounce class and by small brownies – the latter fat and golden but still small brownies. As Michael said 'the big wans is not movin' when thim wee fellers is about' and of course he was right. He usually is.

So we made our way slowly homeward in the afternoon sunshine. The lough was blue now and sparkling and that usually means bad fishing – on that lough at least. However, conditions did not deter us from a last drift outside a tiny grassy islet. Here are more boulders of all shapes and sizes than you can imagine – acres of them in four to five feet of amber water – good sea trout ground and a salmon lie too. And for a bonus we picked up here not far out in the last five yards of a drift a third fish. This one spent as much time in air as in water and if I am quite truthful gave us more sport than either of the others. But he was only about a pound and a half – newly in and crawling with sea lice. And so home.

You may think these fish no great credit to the Loch Ordie but you would be wrong. I know this lough intimately and in very many of its moods and I can assure you that when sea trout are 'off' in this water they are really off and all but uncatchable unless you are looking for finnock. The bigger fish will take well, once settled, for a period – perhaps two or three weeks and will then go off – maybe for a month or more, coming on again in September. Given a suitable day during this 'off' time you will move them only to the dap but in any ordinary wind and wave I would back the Loch Ordie provided it is imaginatively fished with intervals of dragless drifting, short quick pulls and occasional line twitchings or indeed any device that will make the 'fly' simulate some living organism but will not drag it under or swamp it.

And although I have been writing of sea trout, the Ordie on any water containing good brown trout will bring up the best of them.

James' Trout

In my part of Donegal there is never any doubt in conversation about the identity of a fish of the trout family. A little farther north and south they speak of trout and of white trout thus distinguishing between brown trout and sea trout, but ghillies and anglers in my fraternity call a brown trout simply 'a trout' and a sea trout by its own proper name. This is good because in other places again both are referred to as 'trout' which is technically quite accurate but in practice confusing.

You will therefore understand that when James said 'I saw a big trout leppin' under thim branches', I knew he meant a big brown trout and not one of the sea trout for which I was then fishing. This was, so to speak, the first sighting. It was in early September of a notably dry season with a preponderance of heavy all-but-windless days and very low water. Sea trout were almost uncatchable and going stale at an alarming rate. I like the lough low because it normally fishes well when certain offshore reefs carry least depth of water, but entirely happy circumstances are rarely in combination. The drought producing a far-fallen lake usually has its root cause in too much sun and with it there comes too high a water temperature.

It was the sun and the torpidity of the sea trout in the open water which had taken us to the place where James saw the big trout, for there, surrounding an enchanting bay in the wooded lake shores, was deep water close inshore and vast outreaching and ancient oaks – under them deep shade. If it has its attractions, it also has its inbuilt handicaps for a fisherman, this bay, for the reason that its location generally deprives it of whatever wind there may be – hence, of course, the brooding woodlands of heavy oak, hanging lichens and luxuriant fern. Here, deep under the trees a boat can find refuge from a gale from almost any quarter and it is indeed a much frequented retreat of ours. Halfway between a favourite fishing ground and the normal boat landing it's exceedingly useful and I have many times hauled the boat up under the trees and walked home when the lake has been seething with white horses and the reed beds flat from sheer weight of wind. You can get caught out on a big lough however well you know its moods.

I must add, if you are to visualize the place – that this haunt of trout and sea trout – and the odd salmon though it is not truly salmon ground – and of woodcock and badger and fox ashore – runs deep into the hillside through a narrowish neck which all but cuts it off from the open lake. Inside, apart from the dense forest growth fringing the shores there are great lily beds, the home of that rarity the water rail and patches of tall reeds beloved of reed buntings.

The trout are very numerous and mostly small as indeed they are in the lake as a whole. Every spring the salmon trollers out in open water will get the occasional six- or seven-pound brownie – very dark and ugly-headed but generally we call a trout of over a pound a good fish. You get them while sea trout fishing but the really big ones don't rise and years go by without capture on the fly of a fish over two pounds. Not only are they absent from catches but the big trout are seldom or never seen and might not exist, hence our real interest when we see one show, whatever the reason for its appearance on the surface.

In actual fact if you could see the place where James' fish showed you would say 'just the place for a big trout'. The shore is steepish under the trees and in the clear amber water you can see a labyrinth of shattered rocks sliding away into the shadows of unseen depths. Here a big fish can lurk unseen while the small fry shuttle to and fro in the rim of the sunlight filtered through overhead leaves. Truly a wonderful lie for a big trout. I have always thought that good trout must be here because in addition to the normal wind-blown and water-hatched fly life, there is a constant rain of caterpillars and all manner of small insect trout provender from overhead. But the average trout caught here have always belied the fancy and I believe the thought and the hope are by and large ill-founded.

There you have the background and against it I tell a little story with its own lesson in the never-ending series that make up fishing.

Sea trout fishing being as unproductive as I have suggested and the weather too quiet to give us a breeze that would induce stale salmon to move to a fly, I decided to use evening hours to study the area where James' trout had shown and if conditions suited to see whether I could bring him up to a fly. We went out two days later in a pleasantly idle frame of mind making a leisurely passage to the bay across water carrying but the merest crinkle of wave and marked only by the rises of small trout and, in their regular haunts, the dimples of the shoaling char. James shipped his oars thirty yards from our previously agreed observation post and the boat carried her way until we were close inshore and under the trees. A tiny deep inlet probed the woods here and on its distant side a huge oak all but dipped its lowest branch in the water. Here was the 'lie'. The sun had only just dipped but under here it was darkish and warm and the midges were extremely active.

We soon found that in that quiet place a too vigorous slap at the creeping myriads would rock the boat and produce unwanted surges on the dark water. I would like to tell you that we saw a great boil made by our fish or, even more pleasant, that I moved him to a skilfully presented wet fly – but in fact we saw no sign of him and presently, in gathering dusk and midge-maddened, gave up and went homeward. What we did see, as we turned in towards the boat landing was a herd – I use the word deliberately – of big sea trout being shepherded by a very big otter. The fish milled round in unhurried fashion, back fins and tails showing – a very good class of fish which were big enough to be grilse. It looked like a game with neither hunter nor hunted in any hurry and I'm afraid our approach spoilt it.

I kept anticipating a weather change and a week later we did have a small wind from a quarter that would give us a breeze in the bay. We therefore devoted a morning (lest the north wind should act normally and die completely at sunset) to fishing round and about and over our chosen area. We brought back seven fat nine- or ten-ounce trout and saw a very dark sea trout of about five pounds leaping vertically. But James said no – his fish was a trout. I comforted him and myself with the suggestion that after all one could watch for a single fish for a month of Sundays and never see him – especially in a lake where his lie might be anywhere inside half an acre of water. Still, it was a nice morning and I had been fishing hopefully with

Watson's Fancy, Connemara Black and Butcher in 10's on three-pound nylon. But because the waves ran very nicely in under the trees to chuckle among the broken rocks and the wind stirred the overhead cover so briskly, I drifted a furnace-hackled Loch Ordie in on a long line and worked it by twitch and slow draw by turns. It looked, as I intended it should, like a big caterpillar and made a good mouthful for a good fish. All very fine in theory – in practice useless although it was really an ideal place for the Loch Ordie.

Now I know James very well indeed and I knew that he had in fact seen what he said he saw but I was beginning to lose the edge from my enthusiasm. After all, that fish could be anywhere round about the area though it's true big fish normally have a lie and a settled feeding beat. Again and anyhow, he might be and probably was a bottom-feeder and all James had seen was his annual plunge!

The wind, a one-day's wonder, died away again and we had a succession of hot calm days – the lake falling still further but the sea trout as dour as ever. Any fish we did catch were warm to the touch and the water temperature was far too high for fish except greedy little trout to feed at all. But we picked another evening in which, this time, to fish well into the dark and all the way along the wooded bay shore. I tried a small Queen of the Water on the bob and soft-hackled Black Pennells on both dropper and tail and fished them in the calm with very slow fingering and as deep as I could get them. And in two hours, apart from the crash of some crazy salmon plunging out beyond the gloom of the trees, we neither heard, felt, nor saw a fin.

On the way back I told James we'd give it a miss now until we got some real rain or colder winds and a falling water temperature and we did exactly that. To be honest I was beaten in the sense that I simply did not know how to overcome the extremely adverse conditions: as the days went by I almost forgot that trout because salmon fishing began to pick up a little, heaven knows why, and we concentrated on the open water drifts in preference to the fickle and fluky wind draughts of the bay.

And so the last month of the season drifted by until with two days left to fish there came the kind of wind and weather we had lacked since early July. Soft but steady and reasonably strong winds and broken cloud combined in a way that sent us out early in the day along the lee shore of the lough. Here we fished the known salmon lies in a beautifully broken wave that surged up into the waterside ferns. Water temperature was down but not markedly so. There is, by the way, a belief in some quarters that spring-run fish – after months of increasing staleness and refusal to look at a fly – will come on in September. Occasionally they do but in my experience not often enough to justify any great expectation. It was like that, this last fishing day of the season: places which certainly held fish – the pebbly point where the char spawn in the backend and some channels between the rocky islets and lastly a long belt of reeds on a clean sandy bottom – were utter blanks. This belt of reeds lay off the mouth of a smallish river which entered the bay of the trout near where it opened out into the lough and drifting baywards from here in a roughish wave I did have a sullen swirl to the dropper. I went down one size in the fly and we covered the fish again without result.

Light was very good and I have seldom seen better conditions for salmon fishing in that lough. We drifted on into the bay because odd salmon do lie there. Down here at the bottom of the wind the wave was bigger than ever and I went back to the number seven Dusty Miller on the dropper. That change produced a fierce deep take from something very hard pulling and dour. I was fishing 8 pound nylon to suit the fly size and I bent the rod hard to produce at the net in a few minutes, a beautiful brown trout of four pounds which had taken the tail Yellow Torrish. That was a big trout for that place.

It really was an exceptionally handsome fish, well-shaped and coloured, deep and small in the head and it came to the fly about twenty yards outside the big oak. If indeed it was the fish we had been vainly pursuing for so long it had refused every conventional trout fly – sunk or surface and every feathered lure I could think of, to take in the end a biggish salmon fly on a relatively clumsy iron. There must be a moral here but I'm afraid it's a little complicated.

Ashore, later, I gave James the trout. He said, as I knew he would, that he was thankful for it but it wasn't the fish he saw leppin'.

The Yellow Stone

Since I was a boy and the salmon was at once the abiding passion of my life and the greatest mystery of all to me, I have wondered and I still wonder, why the fish in loughs are so strongly attracted to lies by isolated rocks. The decided current of a river acting on and around a rock in that medium will create a microclimate and a lie – so much is readily understandable. Its counterpart, probably bulkier and rising sharply from the lough floor, often in relatively deep water, may provide the element of cover but it is difficult to see what more.

Yet these isolated rock formations, great boulders or segments of reef do gather fish to themselves and there is a scattering of them in most rough country waters in Scotland, the islands and Ireland – some of them famous and the focus of concentrated fishing. Mostly the named ones bear descriptive labels. I know several 'Salmon' rocks, a 'Priest's' rock, a 'Pulpit' rock, a 'Kitchen' rock, a 'Red', 'Black' and 'White' rock and many more. They differ in size, character, colour and in fishability in any given strength and direction of wind. One can find a limited similarity rock to rock in one group – that composed of rocks lying in shallow water. Here the fishing rock can simply be a convenient mark on which to align the drift of a boat and it does not necessarily follow that the stone itself has any special virtue as a lie. It is merely the visible indication of a shallow area which holds fish. Any fish caught within say thirty yards of the rock is said to have been caught 'at the rock', and so it gains in repute until it comes to possess some kind of imaginary magic.

You and your ghillie will look at it through narrowed eyes from afar when salmon are hard to come by and one of you will say, 'There's a nice wave on the Priest's Rock.' Presently you will shift your ground so that you will fish the rock though in your heart you know that when they are 'off' they are as down at the rock as anywhere else.

I said that your true isolated rock rising out of deep water could only qualify as a holding-place on the score of providing some sort of cover, but its underwater contours are hidden and there may be ledges and irregularities quite unsuspected and offering resting-places for salmon. There may be other hidden virtues in such a place – perhaps such a prominent feature of the lake floor comes up in particularly featureless subterrain – or perhaps it acts on underwater currents as it does on surface wind and wave drive. For my part I am content that there are days and occasions when salmon sail flywards from the shadowy depths beside the rock and my faith in the fishing mark finds new justification.

However cynical you may be in a non-taking period, these places do lure you on and the Yellow Stone is no exception; indeed it gains in allure because it is hard to reach. It serves no purpose to tell you exactly where the loch is since it is a private fishing: for my story it is enough to say it lies in a Hebridean waste of mountain and moor – a big sheet of water in a country that seems as much water as firm ground. Here on a bright day of blue sky, innumerable lochs large and small, round and irregular, reedy and rocky, glitter like jewels in a setting of bronze and gold and chocolate of peat, and beyond it all the roaring Atlantic – rushing green over white shell-sand beaches. Without sun the lochs are cold silver or pools of darkness in that most desolate of all landscapes and the melancholy of the Isles comes quickly to the sensitive.

The Yellow Stone lies a hundred yards off the north shore of a low headland, itself at the north end of the big loch. To reach it is a major exercise: one walks, climbs and stumbles over three miles of bad going – a large part of it that most trying of ground, small round boulders hidden in thick grass and heather – to reach the boat. Once afloat there is four miles to go on the outboard motor and because the Yellow Stone fishes best in a north wind that means, in a salmon-suiting wave, four miles of what can be a big head sea. In fact, from a wave-raising point of view the area of the Stone can be worked with an east wind but it fishes badly, like most places, with air from this quarter. So on the rare occasions when we go, we select north wind days, trim the boat carefully and pray that the trough of a wave will not drop us on one of the numberless jagged rocks that litter the channels through the little islands. It can be an interesting passage. Knowing navigation makes use of the fact that some of the islands lie across the north wind and give short interludes of quieter water. Their western and eastern ends, where they terminate in tumbles of boulders, sometimes yield a fish where the wild surge of waves across the point eases slightly as it feels the island's lee. This fishing is for the homeward passage if one has not stayed too long on the distant fishing ground.

We picked a June day, Angus the keeper and I, with half a gale blowing from the north. The light was strong and the sky as hard as a northerly sky can be but you cannot have everything, and our estimate was that across the wide bay to the Stone there would be a strong enough push of wind to build a fishing wave. I think on balance I would rather have a good brisk rolling wave from a wind in an indifferent quarter, than too little wave from a good direction.

Very few systems in the Long Island have spring runs of salmon and the great bulk of the fishing depends on summer fish. June is rather early but at the time I have in mind we had had very high water and fish should be in the big loch. En route to the fishing ground we were reassured by the sight of two plungers, as it happened too far off to mark accurately.

Angus put the tiller over and made a small detour over the approximate location of one of the fish and throttled back while I trailed a long line and a fly for a few minutes as we passed. Either it was a remarkably accurate piece of marking on his part or we were simply lucky because almost at once I was able to say 'There he is' and we both watched, way still on the boat, while a fish swam vigorously after the fly – back and fin and tail tip showing in the wave. He took hard and went down with the fly – a No. 6 Silver Grey and we were 'in him'; Angus cut the motor and we had five minutes of lurching and slopping in a big wave before the net went under a fresh eight-pounder. Foundation for the day!

In some places and conditions, salmon will take a trailed fly very well and there are days when if you elected to do so you could catch more this way than fishing the fly from a drifting boat. I have little time for trolling with a bait but it does no harm to trail a fly in passing from drift to drift. Usually the fish take with a bang but one that follows on the surface can be a problem. He may turn away if the speed of the fly is changed in any way – he may lose interest if it is maintained. One takes one's chances. I have often hooked fish that followed, without coming really close to the fly, by quickly pulling off a foot or so of line and allowing the fly to drop back so that the fish so to speak overran it.

An otter regarded us calmly from an emerald-green patch at the back of the beach as we rounded the big headland into the bay of the Stone and Angus stowed the outboard and took to the oars to give us three hundred yards of quiet approach to our fishing. A diver flew high overhead with a quick kakkering cry of its kind. In the bay the wind was strong and even and blowing fairly on to the beach of the headland – here a lee shore. Half-a-mile away to the north-west the shoreline dipped where the outflowing river left the loch. Fish entering this way have the habit of resting in this bay and especially in the area of the Stone, which today with the loch two feet above normal, was just awash. It was mid-afternoon by the sun.

I took off the big Silver Grey and because I thought it suited the light and water clarity, put on another two sizes smaller for the tail and a Dusty Miller, also an eight, on the dropper. Salmon in this area average less than nine pounds and casts as light as will carry the flies are stout enough – mine was about eight pounds b.s.

Before us, when Angus stopped the boat's forward way, was a long reach of stony shore – stretching to the left into the bay and right out to the headland; we had ten feet of water under us and the Stone – so far hidden – lay somewhere in the hundred yards or so that separated us from the beach. The wave was a fraction smaller than I like but the Dusty Miller, tripping and arrowing the wave, twinkled in the sun; it looked right. In spite of its height the loch water was very clear and I could see the

Silver Grey on the tail in an occasional wave, travelling smoothly like a tiny grey ghost. I felt it had a beckoning look but then I do not quite see things as a salmon does in spite of forty years of hard trying!

One fish at least seemed to like the fly, appearing momentarily in the hollow of a wave as he turned down without apparently opening his mouth; we pulled off and were over him again in two or three minutes expecting to raise and hook him on the Dusty which worked beautifully in the sunlit broken water – he did not come again. 'We'll get one by the Stone,' Angus said. Overside the bottom showed clean stones of all sorts and sizes without trace of silt or algae and twenty yards ahead the huge golden blur that was the Yellow Stone we had come so far to seek. On this day of extraordinarily clear water and light it showed as an enormous flat-topped boulder, a hundred tons perhaps of water-worn gneiss, one corner just awash in the wave hollows. Round it were others, smaller and lying deeper – shadowy humps separated by clefts of darkness – round this loch at least there is ample cover.

I fished the Yellow Stone and all around it with such skill, care and concentration as I can muster and if I know anything at all, I do know this game, this kind of water and these conditions – and I could not move a single fish, much less provoke a taking rise. Although these salmon will not stand much fishing and the first time over is by far the best chance, we persisted for a while – quite fruitlessly. Angus pulled out and away saying things in Gaelic about the Stone while I said them in English. Fresh fish were here but if they were not in the best-reputed lie, where were they?

Along the beach on our left was a small round inlet – a bay within the bay so to speak and fairly in its centre was a pile of rocks, the topmost two feet above the waves and others about it awash. We were drifting without plan now and I kept looking at the rocks. Angus knew what I was thinking and said, 'It's too shallow in there – full of rocks – and if we get in there we'll have trouble getting out – but we'll try if you want.' I wanted.

We bumped twice on the way in but Angus twisted the boat head to wind and wave and I fished island style off the stern. The face of the rock-pile was fished with the tail fly just about touching the stones and this was about as near as we could go. At one moment the stern post would hit a boulder just under the surface and the next there would be three clear feet under the keel. I threw a longer line and fished the right flank of the rocks, then as the boat sidled to the left, the other side. And here among the breaking waves came the good solid pull without sign on the surface. Angus said, as he always does when a fish is hooked, 'That's him.' That fish had us in a bad place and fortunately his move when it came was out to sea and not shorewards where it was impossible to follow. One big advantage of the Hebridean way of fishing by backing the boat down on any lie of limited extent, is that if a fast runner is hooked and goes out, the boat is in the best possible attitude, bow to wind, to follow. We pulled straight out after our fish now. He did one threshing double somersault in a turmoil of broken water thirty yards away but we soon had him in the boat – fifteen pounds and fresh enough for his flanks to carry the red veinings of lost sea-lice.

Angus made a rather rude gesture in the direction of the Yellow Stone as we passed outside it and started the motor; I remembered then that the lunch was still in the bag. We ate it as we swooped and rolled south through the islands with the motor at half-speed. Like most fishing days it *might* have been a big day but I was content enough to look at two fish in the boat – neither from the famous Yellow Stone.

Fishing River Mouths

Almost any angler, whatever his capability, will make for and fish a river mouth and often enough he will ruin his chances by lack of discretion in the mode of attack.

It is true that the point where a river enters a lake or where a tributary enters a main water-course almost always provides good fishing.

The places I have in mind are those where a river strikes a lake shore at an angle and forms a current out into the main body of water. It is not a requisite that the current shall be lively and visible. Very often a vigorous flow loses its apparent push and is dissipated because the shallow shelf, the sill over which it flows, is narrow and in the lake plunges abruptly into the deep. But whether the flow continues to ripple outward across a shallow delta or invisibly across deep water, it will assuredly attract fish – salmon for oxygenation and the promise of further progress upstream, sea trout and brown trout for the current-borne feed and of course the higher oxygen content, in normal conditions.

I can think of one such mouth only among the scores that I know, that does not provide better sport than other areas of the same loch and this one fails because its fish-attracting current is wholly lost over a vast area of extremely shallow stony delta – at twelve inches too shallow to provide lies. The usual lie, at the point where the delta edge falls away into deep water is so extensive and too far from current influence and nearby bouldery shores are more attractive. And even if the entry did attract fish they would be quite unapproachable in such thin water. Something of a phenomenon this place, the point of entry of an important spawning river which draws salmon in very large numbers in November and December but which does not fish at all well. I know – I've spent hours and days in fruitless fishing along its delta edge.

Happily, the ground contours responsible are not often met with and in most situations are such as to concentrate fish in a relatively small area – a basic advantage at times offset by the difficulty of playing hooked fish without disturbing others sharing the taking place. Wind direction and wave drive usually dictate the line of approach as does current strength and width and its degree of persistence out in open water. If banks are steep on either flank of the mouth, and this enables you to merge in your background and the lie is within casting reach, fishing from shore will pay. It disturbs the water least of all. Boat fishing is the reverse because whether you drift or fish at wind dictation into the outflowing stream, i.e. upstream, or whether you fish across it, the boat will approach too closely.

In several places I know a combination of boat and bank approach can be used and this enables one to fish all the water with the absolute minimum of disturbance. Where the volume and extent of current-affected water will permit, I habitually cover the fringes and the area beyond reach from the shore by long casting from a boat gently eased in, stern foremost. If in so doing I hook a fish I take it gently out and away to play it. The outer area covered I go ashore twenty yards or more from the fishing area and come back, well below skyline if this is possible, along the shore. From there I fish all the area close inshore with greased or floating line since by this means I can show the fly as far out as I can feed line on the flowing current. It is impossible to generalize on the detail of tactics of course since no two river-mouths are exactly alike: the lie may be close inshore, far out or on the extreme fringe of the current-rippled water. Brown trout and sea trout tend to hang further out or on the fringe of roily water whilst salmon may easily be in the rough broken water under the rod point. The main thing is to keep out of sight if the lies are inshore or shallow.

So much depends on the nature and contour of the bottom. If the river has, as in many cases, scoured some sort of depression at the point of outflow salmon will use it. Currents work in odd ways and play strange tricks and I have seen a hole the size of a dining table scooped out: not where one would look for it where the current is strongest but twenty yards out in a shelf of hard packed gravel. That has to be fished very cautiously indeed and from the boat, by throwing a long line and never allowing the boat or its shadow to come near to the edge of the lie. The point is that whilst the hole may constitute a holding place, the fish actually are more likely to be on its sloping flanks than in its extreme depths and if disturbed simply sink back and thereafter will not move to the fly. This hole can be crammed with salmon in the spring and for a week or two will provide occasional fresh fish. Later, however, though it continues to hold the densest concentration of fish in a large area of the lough, it produces very little since it's constantly disturbed by boats which are allowed by slap-happy ignorant rods to drift over and spoil it.

Holding places which are very small in area are genuinely difficult to fish if they are unmarked. A known lie beside a projecting rock presents no problem – the rock is a permanent mark and approach to it merely a matter of cautious boat handling. But a small concentrated area – a little bit in a lake floor some way off the mouth of an entering stream demands detailed knowledge of the water and of offshore marks.

It takes a fairish volume of inflowing water to hold fish close to the point of entry of that water. They will gather there at spate time but as the stream falls and entering water becomes little more than a trickle they tend to drift away – a movement less marked, of course, in sea trout and trout than in salmon. Salmon 'belonging' to this stream in the sense that they will eventually run into it and spawn there, may in low water wander hundreds of yards away and for this reason I like and always fish carefully any little bays or stretches of clear shore on either side of the stream mouth. Salmon are wanderers in a limited sense, and are subject to some very local movement with wind direction and water height but once settled they will frequent one area until ready for the final autumn movement upstream.

I know scores of small stream mouths in Irish and Scottish waters which always hold fish in their neighbourhood but which are not worth concentrated fishing at the outflow except when the stream is high. At normal summer level you can step dryshod across most of them. Something can be done, incidentally, to improve the holding potential of such places where, as so often occurs, the outflowing trickle is dissipated through a beach of gravel, by cutting a trench through the gravel in such a way as to concentrate the outflow. You may – I repeat may, because it does not always work – create an outrush of fresh water entering at right angles to the shore line and a certain interceptor of travelling fish which follow the shore. I have done this successfully in Ireland where general clearing and opening-up of stream mouths has been shown during the season to have improved fishing and later to have induced rather more sea trout and salmon to enter for spawning. Not enough attention, in fact, is paid to nursery streams either at mouths or source but this is another subject – we were talking about fishing techniques.

In a corner of a Hebridean loch of my acquaintance, there enters a fair-sized moorland river and off its mouth a salmon and sea trout lie trickier to fish than any I know. There is no problem in finding the lie – it is a bare six feet from shore and consists of a hole perhaps three feet deep and as much in length and breadth: just a small hole in the loch floor. Here salmon lie, not in great numbers – usually one or two fish only. And here lying head to stream they can see any movement on shore. Contours are low in flat moorland and even if you go far upstream and cast a long line from a position in the stream bed, you are seen and presumably the fish drops back and out into the loch. At all events you will not get a rise and you leave not knowing whether you have put the fish down or whether in fact the lie was tenanted at all – the black peaty water tells you nothing. The chances are that the lie was occupied. If, however, by means which I shall outline, you succeed in taking a fish you may go away and return in say, two hours' time, confident in the knowledge that another strange and aggressive fish will by then have moved in. It is a small and highly desirable lie in a loch relatively deficient in lies and there are always fish waiting to occupy it. Two things are absolutely certain to ruin any hope of catching the occupant of the moment: the first is, as I have suggested above, to allow yourself to be seen and the second is to overfish at any one time. Half a dozen casts will suffice because in fact if you are going to get a fish, he will come at the first or second cast across the current and slightly above the lie. The ideal approach requires very nice judgment of line length and boat positioning. Some yards from the actual mouth the shore is backed by a four foot peat bank and the trick is to put the boat's nose in below the bank and from there, with the bank giving some background, throw a long line so that the flies are swept across the lie. This dark looking water is actually very clear and fish do see the cast if you overdo line length.

Fish average not more than seven pounds here and fine tackle is quite practical. A second way of approach is on the opposite side of the mouth but I like this less. Water is very shallow and full of water-worn round stones of all sizes from gravel to small boulders. If you are lucky you can ground the boat in the right place but as often as not she will run a shade one way or the other and grate to a stop in the wrong place. If she hasn't enough way she won't ground but will swing off-current pushed at once: and if she has too much and grounds firmly in the wrong spot, you cannot get off again without disturbing the water. Assuming you are correctly placed, again a long cast across the lie is the method. You can catch sea trout fishing directly up the current from the boat placed offshore opposite the mouth but you will not move a salmon. I have had many salmon from this most challenging place but it took a season or two to learn how – strangers are invariably baffled. They all go too near to the lie.

It seems to me that the need for extreme care in the approach is the key to almost all river-mouth fishing. Even where hollows or holes do not constitute the holding place and the river flows out over a gradually deepening bank of sand or gravel and is entirely open and large in area, there is a problem. Salmon are not shy fish in the general sense – by no means as sensitive as sea trout for example, but they quickly react to movement or shadows when water is shallow.

On seven separate occasions in the last few years I have seen vast congregations of salmon at certain river mouths and it has always looked, from a distance, as if one could hardly fail to have a big day. Fish showed continuously, lunging, head-and-tailing and breaking the surface in a fairly compact mass. The best I have been able to do in these circumstances has been to take two fish – though I once hooked three and lost one. The only possible approach is to back the boat in very gently and then cast as long a line as you can command. If you go one yard beyond the critical point you have no chance with fish mulling round in the shallows and similarly if you fail to take a hooked fish out and away before he really resists. You have much more chance with a few scattered fish – the communal panic-sense in a shoal is very strong. As I say, I am not clever enough to hook more than two or three in such conditions but I have learnt that the first cast if well directed will usually be effective. After that fish is led away, played and boated you must rest the fish, keeping quiet in the boat for, say, fifteen minutes, then you may go in and get another. After that you are straining your luck. Suddenly the fish are no longer to be seen and you could think they had simply 'gone off' or 'gone down' or whatever you care to call the phenomenon we all know, but you would be wrong. The truth is that the shoal has gone right away.

Possibly the best known river mouth in British salmon fishing is Endrick Bank on Loch Lomond and this is a very good example of the vast expanse of sand that a considerable river can lay down where it enters into its loch. The taking place is the indented and tortuous edge of the underwater bank where it slides into the deep, and Endrick Bank, apart from its size, is no different from others having the same features. It contains no approach problem because of its area and the wide scatter of fish – a very good example of this type of river entry. I know another – sweet Lough Fern in Donegal where there is a delta of quite another type. Here the Lennan brings down some quantity of peaty-silt which is deposited evenly through reed beds and out into the lake over a large area. There is no 'bank', no marked edge to the delta for an uncommon reason – the pull of current towards the outflowing lower river which leaves the lough about three hundred yards from the inflow. Thus the whole intervening area is floored with silt borne by the river and born of the decaying reeds – of even depth and despite an element of foulness, greatly favoured by the salmon which are held here by the push of water from one river out into the lough and round towards the other. On a late April day with fresh fish in the lough, this river mouth off and about which conventional drifting can be freely followed, can provide wonderfully good sport.

So too can most river-mouths but I don't know any two which are precisely alike: a first visit to any of them may be fruitless because you must know the bottom contours and their close examination will ruin chances for one day at least. What you learn on that 'wasted' day will dictate the methods of approach in varying winds and will bear directly on results for the future.

'There was a kind of a rage on thim'

Once fish are in you need settled weather for good salmon fishing, and settled weather we had – at long last. Otherwise there was in its beginnings nothing to distinguish this day from any other day in May. The mountains slept aloof in blue haze, harsh rocks hidden. The salty west wind reached us over a cold ocean but the cloud cover was thin and soft – the lake was a shade high but falling quickly. The little green islets held each its throng of fluttering white terns and the grebes watched alert on the reed-bed fringes as we pushed off from the landing. 'Maybe them divvles'll take today – it's a brave mornin',' said Michael.

Being close to the coast in the West of Ireland is not, for a fisherman, an unmixed blessing. It is said that of every quart of rain that blows in from the Atlantic, the west coast will get a pint. So it is that against general mildness of climate you have to reckon with a very great degree of weather unpredictability and the too frequent days of rain alternating with sun which lead to constant fluctuation of water level. It is true that repeated rises in rivers will keep sea trout and salmon running in once the running season has begun but the fish hardly settle and this is especially marked in fish which have run, as in our case, into a lake at the head of, or in the course of, the river system. So you never know – however good-looking the day seems to a mere human – whether a take will be 'on them'.

This day I could only echo Michael's hope but I think the boat knew something we did not, to judge by the way she slapped briskly through the breezy narrows between the islands on the way to our chosen first drift. It was early in the day and I don't look for takers much before noon sun time: for this reason, I always leave the best of the water undisturbed until the sun is high. The plan can be discarded in the face of, for example, an impending violent weather change in which case I should fish the best water at the estimated hour of change – a time/weather phase quite often bringing salmon 'on'.

We began far upwind of the best drifts, working the long straight fringe of a reed-bed where occasionally fish will lie and where later in the year sea trout would be thick. The breeze was a little light here, partly in the lee of a long gorse-clad point and I kept the fly size down to 8 with a Gosling on the dropper and a Golden Olive on the tail. There are two fences here running out from shore through the reeds and for some reason, which I cannot analyse, fish are inclined to lie at the 'seaward' end of each. They were not in evidence this morning but we quickly started to get a good class of brown trout – unwanted and therefore returned but welcome because in this lough their taking is a good sign. You can be sure that you have a good chance of salmon if the better trout are taking and conversely that if the small fry are moving there is little prospect of anything better. In my time I have held and thrown away a dozen opinions as to the explanation of this and remain with the conviction that when big fish are moving about actively the small stuff in self-preservation lies low. Salmon do not tolerate their smaller brethren too readily and when in active mood will chase trout and sea trout from favoured areas. I have seen them do this.

To see, to note and to remember are all so much a part of a fisherman's life and of each of his fishing days that I make no apology for the digression but I do take you back now to the drifting boat.

The reed-bed margins covered, we pulled out and into a downwind line which two drifts hence would put us over the best water while at the same time giving us a view over the entire area so that any plungers – rather rare on this lough where fish seldom show – could be seen and marked. The sight of fish rising 'to themselves' is at least an indication that they are not somnolent in their lies. In the event the next two drifts were fruitless and we moved out into deep and unspoilable water while I changed up to sevens in the flies and with the brightening day and fresher breeze to my favourite pink-hackled Dusty Miller on the dropper. We now had good conditions – a nice clear but soft light and a beautiful marching wave pushed by that ever-to-be-cherished thing – an absolutely steady wind. The day looked better and better and now we were coming up to the time that normally and in most places offers the best chance.

The water that held all our hopes needs some description. Here, in a bay of a low scrub-clad shore and stony beach, enters the lough's main feeder river – a considerable stream, born in the mountains and up there dark and peaty. Lower down it cuts through glacial drift, loses some of its peat stain and carries a great load of silt and pebbles. The latter are deposited close by the river mouth where they form a bar while the lighter detritus goes further into the lake to form the delta which is the main gathering place for salmon. The final deposit is a long ridge of sand about a hundred yards offshore. The river-borne small stuff settles on a hard bouldery bottom and the net result is a clean well washed mixture of water-worn stones of all sizes, with here and there open patches of golden sand. Better holding ground for salmon there could not be. Depth goes from a few inches over the bar when the lough is down, to ten feet about a hundred yards out and the best of the delta has no more than four to five feet at this stage. Every fish in such water sees the fly.

Out of the corner of my eye as we started the critical drift I saw a fish surface in what might have been part of a cruise – thirty yards downwind and to our left. Michael was silent but I knew he had seen it because he moved the boat a few yards inshore to bring us, in due course, over the fish. The rise when it came, took me by surprise since it was some way from our mark but the fish made no mistake and had turned down so fast that he was hard-hooked without conscious action from the rod. Then, as so often happens, he seemed almost unaware that he was held and merely moved easily and uncertainly for a moment. He was so quiet that we thought he would lead without trouble and Michael started to pull slowly off-shore, the fish coming quietly for twenty yards or so. That didn't last long, however, for he suddenly turned aside and made a short but violent run with much yanking and head shaking. I held on and we started again when he quietened down. A few yards more and he turned about and bolted back inshore pulling so hard that I had to give line. A run of forty yards or so ended with violent lashing on the surface during which we saw a broad tail much bigger than average. 'Man, he's a rare boy,' said Michael, and clearly we had a good fish: he came tamely enough after that and we soon had him in the boat – about fifteen pounds – a cock with about three weeks in the lake faintly showing on his scales. He had taken the Olive on the tail.

The west wind blew steadily and the waves had the soft gleam that distinguishes a good fishing light from the hard one that puts a metallic sparkle on each uplifted crest. We had need to be fishing again for the take might not last and on dour loughs you make the most of your chances. So we were back on the drift, cast knots checked and boat tidied inside five minutes. I didn't think that the fish we had boated was the one we had seen showing, unless the latter had changed his position. Michael thought him the same fish.

So arguing we covered the last few yards of the drift again and were thinking of moving when a fish arched a very brown-looking back in the hollow of a wave and between two sunken boulders showing golden in the clear water. At one moment I could see the tripping Dusty quite clearly and then it vanished, the line drew taut and the hook lodged somewhere very firmly. A long sub-merged ridge, of which the boulders were part and continuation of a rocky spur ashore ran out here and across it went the fish in shallow broken water. This was awkward: we could not follow but must first pull straight offshore and across the wind while the fish ran downwind. Backing was visible before we could drop down on him and shorten line again but we presently had him on a short line and being led tamely out into safe deep water. Two or three turns of the reel woke him up out there and we had another run, a jump and a dangerous somersault before I had him sliding quietly to Michael's waiting net. How the hook stayed in during that somersault I don't know, for it fell from the fish as the priest was applied. Odd things happen in fishing. This fish looked like about

eleven pounds and a very fresh hen. I mounted a new cast
but used the same flies.

There was a small section of good water still unfished
in the same general area. It lay inshore of the straight line
of drift we had been following – a shallow bay, sand-
floored and grassy margined and separated from the outer
water by the half-submerged skeleton of an ancient dead
tree rising starkly from the water. Salmon tend to hang
about the jungle of submerged timber – we have had
many fish hooked within feet of the branches. To extract
an active fish from this danger area calls for good co-
ordination between rod and boat-handling – something
like a combination of light but firm holding and a quiet
progression by gentle smooth oar strokes out into snagless
water. If a fish resents being led and turns directly back
with any sort of vigour you've lost him.

It was after one o'clock by the sun as we approached
the tree and I was confidently looking for a take all the
way down that short drift but we passed on and into the
downward corner of the bay without seeing anything.
There, however, within feet of the rusty trailing wire
cutting off a shallow cattle drink, there was a little white
flash of foam such as a trout makes in drowning a floating
fly and we had another fish. He came out of the bay like a
lamb, pulling evenly and moving steadily beside the boat
and under the rod. A fish can go on doing this indefinitely
and out in safe water Michael turned the boat sharply to
get us away from him: some line went out but with no
great strain and I found I could bring the fish up easily. As
he rolled and splashed at a safe distance he was awkward
rather than strong and we saw that he was small, and on
the dropper. In the net he looked like a grilse but even the
more precocious of that ilk do not arrive in this lough till
late June and, in fact, he was a true spring fish as his scales

later that day showed – but he was a bare five pounds in weight. We have a sprinkling of these very small fish every season. I *think* – but I am far from *knowing* that they begin as exceptionally small smolts at migration – fish which do not overcome their inbuilt handicap during sea feeding. It is difficult otherwise to understand why, visiting sea feeding grounds in company with others which make up to an average of ten pounds, they put on so little weight. Or do they stay inshore with the sea trout and grow up on the relatively poor diet of the estuaries? Some salmon do this, notably on the coasts of Newfoundland where fish from a number of rivers seem to spend their sea-life close inshore: they are visible on the surface and feeding in the estuaries. Their native rivers are known as small fish rivers and the local belief is that the fish are stunted because they fail to move as far afield as the rich feeding grounds of the average salmon.

We went back into the bay because we had not fished its downwind and easterly point. This is a famous place, for the tail of a glacial drumlin tapers down into the water and continues as a line of boulders far out into the lough making ideal holding ground. Many of the boulders are awash at average summer level and fish will take between and about them. The surge and break of waves keeps fish on the move on a day when you have the right wind. But it can be a slightly irritating place to fish because your fly must alight on or close to the stones and whilst a hook-up is easy enough to free, you end with very dull hooks.

A dipper sat bobbing on one of the stones today as Michael pulled slowly along the line and I fished into the surge. We were talking about the rarity of the bird here on the lake and far from the shallow running water he loves, when I fouled a boulder with the tail fly fixed firmly and apparently immovably. Michael backed down on it while I merely held on lightly. But the 'boulder' moved out to meet us, passed the boat and headed out along the submerged point so smartly that I had to stand and hold the rod high to keep out of trouble. That fish had sixty or seventy yards off the reel in a flash and finished with a magnificent plunge in a shower of spray. His subsequent tactics belied the promise – he settled down to slow stubborn pulling and try as I would, he simply would not come up – just a dour head down plugger. Side strain eventually got him off balance and he came to the net – bright shining and about eight pounds, a lovely little cock with a tiny head and thick wrist.

The west wind blew as steadily as ever and I don't know which gave me the greater joy – the expanse of the softly-lit lake, its limits lost in the woods at the mountain's foot – the bright green of the reeds and the gleam of golden sand near at hand – or the four fish lying in the boat as witness to our understanding of the salmon fisher's craft.

'Michael,' I said, 'we've had our share – we'll go home,' and home we went. But I must tell you that casting idly as we rowed upwind, heading straight for the passage through the islands I hooked a fifth fish, another fresh one which we played until, as he came to the net, the hook simply came away. We watched him turn down, gleam golden twice or thrice and vanish. However much we had wanted him his freedom would have left us, as it did, without regret. We wished him luck.

It was two-thirty and clearly fish were still in something of a taking humour and I think that persistent fishing would have given us two or three more. But we had seen an hour or two when they really were keen on the fly. Michael had the last word as we walked up from the boat, 'Man,' he said, 'there was a kind of a rage on thim!'

Lure of the Big Lough

The big water, whether lake or loch or lough, according to country, ideally is enfolded by mountains. They should be close here and distant there and, guarding your playground, familiar to you. Islands should be there too with windy straits between and favoured drifts among them and the whole a delight to eye and mind on days of sun and storm alike: in total, a magnificent challenge to your fisherman's instincts.

There is a special quality, coming near to a magic of its own belonging alone to the fishing of a really big sheet of water. The fine mechanics of presenting a fly in such a place are no different from those employed on your smaller loch, but the whole business of taking a fish from a veritable waste of water contains a vastly greater satisfaction and a special joy if you've a mind to act on a compound of knowledge and instinct.

Every sheet of water large or small offers a challenge but it will always be less daunting if you look at it *as an area of ground covered by water*, and you will not really succeed until you know that ground. True, you cannot walk it but you can study it by scrutiny of surrounding contours, by map or chart study, by sounding line and in some cases, by just looking over the side of your boat. And it takes a long time, using all or any of these ways of learning, to know a big lough. When you do you can use reasoned fishing tactics based on knowledge and, possibly most important of all, on instinct for times and places, weather and the probable moods of fish in those places and at those times. This is the precious freedom of the lough: no-one can confer it on you – you have to earn it the patient and the thoughtful way.

It gives you the *probable* answer to that problem which is so much greater than on a small water – where in all that wide expanse, in all those miles – a fish or better several fish, may be found, raised to the fly and boated. And this mark you, in an infinite range of conditions.

I have wondered whether the appeal of the big lough resides for me in the beckoning of distant places – the far-off drifts looking fishiest so to speak and I admit there may be a tiny grain of substance in this. But the width of choice is surely the prime attraction however the motives may merge one into the other. The great elements are wind and weather which can narrow or widen the choice of fishing ground according to the lie of your lough and the character of its shores, its bays and headlands. It is certain however that so long as boat movement place to place is not totally weather-inhibited, there will be some scope for the following of instinct, some ability to proceed afloat at the bidding of the inspiration of the day. It is then that basic knowledge comes into play so that wind and weather can be made to serve your purpose rather than to result in a wasted day or a journey to an untenable fishing ground. True, big lakes breed their own often very changeable weather and there can be mischances – totally unpredictable changes of wind, for example, which can reduce the best-laid plans to the status of a nonsense. On the credit side however the big water affords scope for contingency planning to cover some such events.

If, by way of illustration I take an imaginary day on the big lough on which I spend some months of each year, you may be sure that it is a reflection of fact showing the kind of appraisal of chances both of weather and of fishing success, that must be made before one takes boat. And I should say now that we don't always do that – there are days when close inspection of the lough does away with any hope of fishing. Foolhardiness has no place in fishing any big open water and when a gale makes boat launching difficult, you retreat and return later or on another day. It happens to me rather rarely because from my quarters I can see clearly with good binoculars a certain rock in a bay half-a-mile distant. When the wave breaks white on the rock I know that all but very limited and generally unproductive fishing grounds are inaccessible until the wind falls or shifts direction because in existing conditions we should be operating along a lee shore where the wind would blast down to us after an over-water reach of several miles.

In all other conditions there is a conference on the beach before we start. The first query – where are most of the fish lying? we answer easily from recent experience, the second is almost as simple. What parts of the holding areas will fish best with the wind where it is and at its observed strength? This also we can answer from intimate knowledge and the mental picture it gives us of just how that area will look today. But the feeders are running hard and the lough is up two feet since yesterday – will the fish have moved? It's early in the season and while inflowing fresh water will assuredly draw some fish, there will not be the general shifting of ground that you would find in September. So Murphy's Bay and Sandy Bay should be our objectives and the time now is eleven by the sun. We have a pull of about two miles and the best fishing time is from twelve till two so that we can do it. So far so good but there is a last and important consideration – will the weather hold? At existing weight of wind there is no problem. We shall have a following breeze on the way out, good wind and wave on our fishing ground and no real trouble to get back in the evening – *if it doesn't blow up*. What if it does blow up – how do we cover that contingency? – beach the boat, walk three hundred yards to the road and get Pat Murphy and his car to bring us home. Right, then that's it and we'll go. You will observe that the great thing in all this is to be able to visualize conditions as they will be some miles away – that comes from knowing your lough.

On another day with another wind and let us say, much less wind and wave, we shall be calculating which of the promontories are holding fish where they shelve into the deep and of those which will catch that whisper of breeze. Maybe if it turns out that we have too small a wave for salmon, it will be enough for sea trout so we need a long gravelly point that is also a sea trout lie. This is no problem since we know them all, have fished them recently, and can make a reasonable estimate of the density of fish.

It's important in this latter context to know the travelling routes of fish in the days immediately following a run and it's nowhere as vital as in the big lough. Both sea trout and salmon travel in companies which persist for a few days after entry and they will have staging places where they're inclined to rest while travelling. True, odd fish take up permanent lies almost anywhere but the bulk of them will pass long stretches of likely-looking shore without pause and will frequently settle for a short time in places of which the attraction is a mystery. But it's our business to know first the travelling route – usually fairly

close inshore – and second the resting places. These may
be and usually are, quite different from the permanent lies
which numbers of fish together will occupy until they
move upstream into a feeder in the late autumn. In a big
lough therefore you must be able to anticipate salmon and
sea trout behaviour as conditioned by the physical features
of the bottom and the shores. Without a guide you could
waste days and weeks fishing non-holding areas. In a
small lake even without local knowledge, persistent fishing will bring some results – not so in the bigger waters.

You are always pitting your skill against nature in the
actual process of fishing, but it is an infinitely more
rewarding exercise in every way when that skill is used
successfully at a place and time and in conditions of your
own choice – a choice made in the light of experience and
with an instinctive recognition of the best chance each day
has to offer.

I know of no greater joy in fishing than the curious
attraction of a long passage to some distant drifts to catch
estimated conditions just right and to get one's salmon.
You study the lough as you go. You were right to avoid
the easterly grounds because there you can see, flashing
white in the far distance, the broken white water and
high-flung spray, while in the extreme lee of the shore
you now follow, the deep bays show still and spruce dark
under the wooded mountain. A skiff of rain slats against
your oilskins and across the mouth of the big bay the
wind has a long sweep and here there's a nice rolling wave
– but this is not salmon ground and you go on. You hear,
high above, the hoarse voice of the morning raven on
some dark errand of his own. That mallard on the outer
island has hatched her brood and there they are, a line of
frantic paddling morsels bobbing like corks behind the
duck. The otter that uses that turf-capped white boulder

for dinner table had a fish last night and two hoodie crows are pulling at what the otter left. A disturbed fish plunges behind the boat as you cross a patch of shallow water and your once-distant fishing ground is in sight now and beckoning you on.

Lough of the Big Wind

The glen runs east and west. It draws wind prevailingly from the Atlantic, compresses it between its two-thousand-feet-high walls and releases it where they recede, to blast half the County of Donegal. Just so long as there is some west in a gentle stir of air along the mountainsides, there will be a steady fair breeze in the glen – a strong wind over that geologically tortured landscape will transform a haven of summer mountain grandeur into a shrunken world of screaming gusts.

The floor of the glen is occupied by a narrow winding lough – a considerable area of water which because of the steepness of the hillsides has few shallow shores along its length but a big beach and fan of sand where the river enters at the western end. The water, coming off rock rather than peat, has very little colour and out from the lough head beach one can see the clean sand bottom for hundreds of yards in any direction. This forms the main, almost the only, fishing area and as the season advances carries a big stock of sea trout and some salmon. The fish gather here because until they move into the river to spawn in autumn floods, they cannot get further. One branch of the little head river comes down a high cliff face not far from the lough and no fish can go higher in this arm of the river; the other quickly peters out. Fish come from the sea up a boisterous river famous for its salmon, through a big lough where many again are caught, and finally through a second river, sluggishly meandering through boggy moorland to enter the lough of the big wind. Here in rarely disturbed and carefully guarded water, there can be superb fishing. Days there are favours to a very few, but the real problem is the weather – the plan to fish has to be the plan of the day only, finalized when the weather of the day can reasonably be judged. Even then to judge from a distance is to gamble heavily; one can start out in a near calm and find a rising gale on arrival and on one occasion at least this happened to me. You shall judge whether my gamble was lost or won.

This was the way of it. I had been mixing sea trout and brown trout fishing and getting pleasant little bags of browns and twos and threes of sea trout in a rough unseasonable August. The salmon in the lake were stale and dark and the lily-pads were thick along the edges of the reeds. Salmon and lily-pads do not belong together and the spring fishing ground had an unreal look despite the plunging fish. About the middle of the month I had a great urge to get among the sea trout, in a place where I could open my shoulders and cast a line. I love little rivers but I was weary for the moment of rock-climbing on their banks and of creeping through tangled gorse and wet fern. I wanted to sit out on a big lough and fish. Dedicated lough fishers will know what I mean – the heave of the boat, slow talk with the ghillie and a tripping bob-fly to watch.

We picked a day when, down in the village, the slender tips of the ash trees barely moved and the blue turf smoke just drifted, and by mid-morning we were tugging the boat foot by foot down some yards of very sticky yellow sand. The lough of the big wind was steel-grey under grey clouds but there was no more than a nice sea trout ripple over the fishing ground when we pushed off. Wind was offshore and directly down the lough. I had my eleven-foot cane and a 7lb cast with two flies which I think were Silver Doctor and Golden Olive. I am not sure, but it matters not at all because they did not bring a single rise though John worked the boat cunningly in short diagonals across the shallows. A remarkably bold stag stared at us from the shore and I thought how he fitted his background – the heather at the back of the beach, the ancient wind-contorted pines in twos and threes behind that, and the mass of other trees dark against the pale rock of the mountain.

John came back over the water we had fished and started a fresh series and now with four feet of water under us I began to look for fish: the best I could find was a single pounder. We had now been once over about a quarter of the fishing area and it was clear that something was amiss. Something was, as the next few minutes showed because the weather broke as suddenly as it can among the high hills. The rain came first – biting cold rain that sent us quickly into tightly-buttoned waterproofs – and hard on its heels the wind. In minutes we had a salmon wave in place of the light ripple and the blast through the tossing pines seemed to be growing. 'John,' I said, 'we shall be lucky if we are not blown off before we've fairly started.' And my ghillie, who holds this place in something like awe, good rough-water man as he is, put the boat in while we found a long, narrow, heavy stone which, with the very long mooring line knotted round its middle, went in the bow. I left the tail fly where it was but put a rather big Zulu on the bob. It was the type of Zulu I like with really wide silver tinsel prominent along the body. My diary is lacking in that it fails to record the size but I think it was a seven – which makes it a big Zulu. I thought that once waterlogged it would hold the cast down in the big blow that by all the signs was coming.

The next working line across the narrow head of the lough found us about forty yards off the beach and I would say that wind and wave were enough but not too big. I rose fish after fish mainly in the pound to pound-and-a-half class and we netted three of them. The Zulu was too big for this water and the class of sea trout we were finding, but the best drifts were yet to be fished farther out, and there the wave was bigger and the bulky fly might come into its own. Still the wind grew, and worse, was becoming squally. We put the boat head to wind and John held her in very short drifts while I fished off the stern. The stone in the bow kept her stable but every now and then would come a blast that moved us bodily, flattening and blackening the water before chasing away down the lough to whip the tops off the waves as it gathered momentum. In one of the gusts I found myself playing a rather better fish – two-and-a-half pounds – which I had to net because John dare not let the boat go. Conditions were becoming downright unpleasant: in the squalls the bitterly cold driven rain stung our hands and everything in the boat streamed with water. The line shot sluggishly as very wet lines do and the cast felt soft. There were fewer rises but those sea trout that did come up meant to take and the Zulu accounted for two more of about two pounds each.

That gave us seven and I looked at them slithering to and fro in two inches of rain water and decided it would be kind to John to call it a day. I twisted round and made appropriate gestures to him but he shook his head and motioned towards the bow with a jerk of his chin. We

were no more than fifty yards off-shore but it took five
minutes of hard pulling before the boat grounded. Hands
partly dried on ends of scarves, we somehow got cigarettes going but they were quickly sodden and cast away.
John untied the stone in the bow and measured the line:
there were about seventy yards of it and it was almost
new.

To our left and opposite the start of the unfished water
was a solitary pine rooted in the edge of the heather and a
bare two yards from the water's edge, and to this, low
down, John secured the free end of the line. As we settled
in the boat again we were struck by the most appalling
squall. It roared through the pines behind us and out over
the lough, picking off the tops of the waves and, while we
watched, lifting solid sheets of water high over the shoreline trees. Two-thirds of the glen was obscured by low
cloud, driving rain and water torn off the lough. No boat
could have lived in it.

I thought we might become airborne at the end of our
rope and I was sure of it if we ever swung broadside on.
John said, 'Holy Biddy!' as we sailed out, dug his oars in
hard and put his back into retarding our slide till our
mooring came taut. When it did we were reasonably
steady but swinging with a most disconcerting motion in
a wide arc. I lifted the rod and fed some line to stream out
in the gale, lowered it to parallel the water and worked
the fly by simple movement to the right. The fly did not
work – it merely travelled along waves and hollows –
mostly rather deep. It suddenly stopped dead and I was
into something – either a big sea trout or a salmon. I had
not seen any break in the wave rolling away from us, nor
the fish, and after two or three minutes decided we had a
big sea trout. There was no salmon play in this fish – he
was down on the bottom, surging about and pulling hard

but not going far away. I dare not lean too hard on him because the boat swung like a pendulum when we suffered an extra buffet from the wind and I found myself leading the fish across the stern. The boat pitched hard, kicking up her stern and constant strain adjustment was necessary because the fish seemed to hug the bottom and did not rise to the upswing of boat and rod one little bit. John kept rowing hard to ease the pull on our lifeline and I hung on to whatever kind of fish we had.

I could not time the play but I suppose ten minutes, which seemed like half-an-hour, went by before he began to tire and presently came up in the trough of a wave on a short line. I had a vision of a light-brown back, fin and tail and profuse spotting on the body. His head was up and I increased strain to keep him coming, John shipped oars and put out the big net all in one smooth movement. We had him. I tried to look round but was instantly blinded by the rain; I heard the stretcher unshipped for use as a priest and then the thud of its application. The oars stayed inboard and we began to creep shoreward as John heaved on the straining line. When the boat grounded and he lifted the bows on to solid sand, I did look round to see, still in the net, a magnificent brown trout. Darker than he looked in the water, he was nevertheless golden and shining and vividly spotted – a little coarse in the head like all big trout in waters of that country but a very handsome fish. He had the Zulu. Six pounds, we said, and six pounds and two ounces he actually was.

We put the rod and loose gear where it would not be whisked away by the gale and using oars for rollers dragged the boat up the wet sand to the heather where in a little gully we strapped her down keel uppermost and with lacings of rope anchored to heavy stones. The day was over – in a weather sense a bad one with more of early March in it than of August. The fish were thrown hastily into the bag and we made for the shelter of the rhododendron thickets en route to the car to shed the wet clothing, get warm again and light cigarettes in comfort. This to me is always one of the blessed moments in a bad day.

As for the gamble, well, I suppose it came off. On the one side seven sea trout and a big brown, on the other such a buffeting and such an element of hazard as only the lough of the big wind – and one other that I know – can give.

On Being a Fisherman

To me, the finest of all fishing stories is that told of Thomas Tod Stoddart who, met by a friend enquiring as to the master's current occupation said, 'Man, I'm an angler'. This is so utterly right for that man and those like him know precisely what he meant.

It's being like Stoddart – being a dedicated angler that leads one to the little brooks, the spawning rills, in the chill of winter in the hope of seeing a waving tail in the thin flow over bright gravel. Such a small thing – but enough to stop an angler's heart in the close season. In the lane passing my cottage a culvert under the road carries a runnel of water almost too small to be called a brook and there the other day, on one of my frequent visits, I saw two spawning sea trout of about a pound – in four inches of water and a dozen miles from the river. I watched these fish for a long time and still remember them with a small warmth of heart. Of no significance to most people they are important to me.

The vocation of being an angler is filled with unending interest but it has to be, and often truly is, an attitude of mind and a consequent way of life. It is this which distinguishes your true fisherman from those who throw an occasional line and are interested in a limited sense. The question can be one of opportunity of course, and it would be unkind to ignore that possibility. To languish in an industrial city when your heart is by the river or on the moorland is indeed a wretched thing. But I have been wondering how much fishing there would be in those islands without the dedication of the confirmed angler, and for that matter – how much of that part of general nature conservation that is linked with fishing and fishing places would exist without him.

You see, I don't believe that a man can be the kind of fisherman whose life is fishing and the places to which it takes him without having and discharging a responsibility which is specially his. He is absorbed not alone in the manipulation of the tools of his craft but in the entirety of his world and this involves his relationship to all nature – above and below water. He has, of course, in his, the quietest of pursuits, unequalled opportunity for observation of many things that the most ardent of ambling amateur naturalists must miss. And his interests will take him abroad at all hours and seasons, rod-equipped or not. Of all men he is likeliest to have his living world kinships in proportion. I have, I must admit however, met men who fished – they were not my kind of angler – and were greedily and ignorantly intent on the destruction of all otters, all herons and all so-called enemies of the fish, even down to the kingfisher. The same men could make a clean sweep of riverside trees for their own convenience and so take shade and cover away and ruin looks and seclusion of many a pool. I know, I have seen it done. Sometimes it is more often ignorance which leads to destruction of an amenity or of wild waterside life. The result can be inexpressibly saddening – the permanent loss of something once seen, heard and enjoyed.

Your true fisherman's attitude of mind will not lightly permit these things and many of his school are actively doing everything within their power to discharge the responsibility which understanding of wild nature enforces on a man who lives as close to nature as he does. His basic relationships are right.

Attitudes in this context, depend, after all, on what a man thinks he is – some superior being with the right to crash round in an environment which is his to destroy – or a partner with animals and birds and all living things in a world in which there are in fact no exclusive rights whatsoever. The fisherman finds no joy in being the most vicious predator of all – in being the element most wholly out of balance. Quite the reverse, a substantial part of the joy of being a fisherman in the fullest sense of the word is the knowledge and ability to cherish and defend the living world which is in acute need of care.

The things a dedicated interest in fish and fishing rest upon have timeless value, the smell of clear running or wave-tossed water, the sight and sound of birds and animals, the wind scents of mountain and woodland, the grace of yellow flag and dipping willow, the lovely vigour of running fish, the elegance of an Olive new-hatched, and the marvel of life in the shallows on a clear lake shore – a whole world, indeed, in our hands and a very old world too.

The breaking of waves on the shore of some lake of trout, secluded, mountain girt and unsullied. And on the beach a driftwood fire bright and blue of smoke – just so might have been the plume from primeval fires in this ancient place. The swan sits yonder, when you look closely, on a nest of bones discarded on the islet by men who seven thousand years since, lifted hands to the blaze as I do now. And they doubtless drank, like me, from the spring there – pure water welling from the rock. Scudding cloud brings spatter of rain and the wind blows as it did all those years ago – wind and rain and fire and water – elemental things to a small creature, like me, crouched among changeless rocks. Yet this is my world and in it, coming towards the end of a long life curiously tied to and always loving the wild places, I am conscious that here in the meaning of this place, are the roots of my philosophy and the faith in all of my fishing.

'Goodbye Now'

Not farewell, but goodbye now, the parting word that is a timeless re-welcome and in the tone of it a benison and a wish for the days to come. They don't like parting with people to whom they say 'goodbye now' in the country where I hear it so often and it has its own little warmth of memory for me.

A fisherman, if his heart is in it, is a man happy in many blessings not least of them a retentive memory. The retained image is not always of great fish brought to net, of this or that stratagem, but of mountain, river and lake and their weather, of creeping and winged things, of water plants and grasses and trees and the honey smell of gorse and the crying of oyster-catchers, of good companions and of places. Small things have great import as components of the whole that makes a fisherman's world. In them reside many of his greatest joys and afterwards they put colour to the canvas of recollection so that scenes in detail come at once to life again. Being part of the immediate background is part of the craft of fishing and of the process of catching fish but there is a wider background which belongs to places and atmosphere of places. You fish in the western isles and you fish in a world where the ocean is at your shoulder – you share the surge of wind and wave with the seals on the skerries, the soaring eagle and the shining salmon that carry a tang of salt far into the hills. You will always have the gold of the tangle at the back of your eyes, the machair of a million flowers and a network of tideways and lochs to lure you as it drew the Norsemen for other reasons 'west over sea' a thousand years before you. You probably catch a great many fish and some part of your fisherman's joy will come at the end of each good day. The rest is in what the Islands have given to the living day and the memory of it.

Fish in my beloved Donegal and in the west is the same wild ocean creaming below vaulted cliffs and the loveliest mountains in Christendom on one hand or the other as you go about your fishing. No eagles here but all else and for added benison such flame of gorse, such fragrance of bog-myrtle and such blue of distant hill as surround no other place of angling. The past, turbulent and gentle too, is close to you here with the legendary thousand Champions of Aileach each in his leather cloak, and the prince-priest Columbcille, the dove of the churches and founder of Iona. Even if you have no taste for ancient Irish history the name of Columbcille is everywhere about you as you fish – by this lough in 521 his birth-place, by this stream the ruins of the abbey where he was taught, this lough bears his name and so does that glen. Here are lonely loughs and brawling rivers, salmon and sea trout and trout, heather and myrtle and the tossing plumes of bog-cotton on ice-moulded moorlands mile upon mile and over all the wild wind from the western sea. This country is steeped in myth and in early history and it bears the very air of it: you do not fish less effectively because the past is at your elbow and hereabouts, only yesterday.

Yes, the essence of places is truly in the air about them and all the life that is in them, to be felt and seen and remembered as you tread softly in your fishing.

A good day with the grilse is a thing to be cherished so rare is it, yet of my good days with the small salmon, I recall as immediately as with the fish of that tumbling little Irish river, the royal fern that here grows waist deep on the banks – such fern as I have never seen elsewhere. Osmunda grows small in my Devon garden; passing daily, I see it through the mist of spray from a roaring brown river and the lovely slim shapes of the grilse laid among the fronds.

Salmon fishing in Donegal is like no other to me. The fish are strong, rough fighters and in the lough hard runners after the hooking. In that country they fit their background bringing the restless life of the sea to an untamable landscape and bearing tradition more akin to the lawless pursuit of salmon in dark roaring waters, than to any refined sport of salmon fishing. Sunlit loughs and zephyrs of summer belie the fancy but your true Donegal days are the wild ones when the boat lurches in the rolling wave on a stormy lee, the great whooper swans, north-bound, call overhead and the spring salmon new from the tide will – and you lucky – give you the run of your life. All of your perceptions are heightened by the very breath of this sort of fishing and you see everything in its designed place, the streaming lace of the mountain water-fall alike with the neat quillwort growing in the lapping waves on the lake shore, the scuttering take-off of tufted duck and the crow and herring gull squabbling over a long-dead lamb among the driftwood on the shore.

You could, if you were very sensitive, find pity for Columbcille far in Iona from this very land he so loved, those fourteen-hundred years ago. I think I know a little, a very little, of what must often have been in his mind – looking across the green rush of the sea to Ireland; and I too in my travels in a new and strident world, have been sick at heart for the crying of the gulls round an island in a lough of Donegal.

'Goodbye Now'

Sources

From *Salmon and Seatrout in Wild Places* (1968): 'The Point
– A Hebridean Day', 'Rough Weather', 'The River Mouth
– Another Hebridean Day', 'Attitudes and Conservation'
(part)

From *Newly from the Sea* (1969): 'Attitudes and Conservation' (part), 'Irish Interlude', 'Salmon at Dusk', 'Lough
of the Crannog', 'Days from the Diary' (part), 'Flies of the
Wild Shore', 'The Yellow Stone', 'Lough of the Big
Wind', 'Goodbye Now'

From *Ways of Fishing* (1972): 'March Day', 'After the
Storm', 'The Finest Moment in Salmon Fishing', 'Days
from the Diary' (part), 'Fishing River Mouths', 'There
was a kind of a rage on thim', 'On Being a Fisherman'

From *Game Fishing Tactics* (1974): 'Weather Change',
'James' Trout', 'Lure of the Big Lough'